mediumship

 a beginner's guide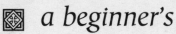

mediumship

 a beginner's guide

LEO GOUGH

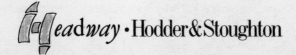

Headway · Hodder & Stoughton

A CIP record for this title is available from the British Library

ISBN 0 340 68009 1

First published 1997
Impression number 10 9 8   7 6   5 4   3 2
Year   2000 1999 1998 1997

Typeset by Transet Limited, Coventry, England.
Printed in Great Britain for Hodder & Stoughton, a division of Hodder Headline plc,
338 Euston Road, London NW1 3BH by Cox and Wyman Limited, Reading.

CONTENTS

Chapter 9 Avoiding frauds and
self-deceivers

Useful Addresses

Further Reading

Glossary

INTRODUCTION

This book is an introduction to the methods and beliefs of mediums. Mediumship is very old and very widespread – as far as is known, mediumistic practices have existed amongst all the peoples of the world since the earliest times – long before the inventions of writing and farming. Although the practices are so widely known, it is very noticeable that the explanations of the unseen world are extremely variable. I believe that this is because the states of mind in which mediumistic experiences can occur are not well connected with the part of ourselves which speaks and thinks articulately. Perhaps the 'mediumistic' part of ourselves existed before the thinking/talking part developed.

Since there are so many different groups practising mediumship, I should explain that this book is a 'New Age' introduction to mediumship.

So what is the New Age? There isn't much that is new about it – it is just a name for a collection of movements, practices and ideas which have all been around for a very long time. One way to define the 'New Age' is to say that it is an attempt to improve the life of human beings and our relationships with the rest of creation, and that within the New Age movement there are many ways of achieving this.

If you become a practising medium, you will have to come to terms with the responsibility of helping and advising your clients. Take this seriously. Some of the people who will come to you will be desperate for help, and if you cannot give them what they need you should pass them on to someone who can.

Although mediumism is not a religion it inevitably deals with the same existential questions that religions try to answer. The most

prominent of these is 'What happens to us when we die?', but
equally important are:

- Who am I?
- What am I doing here?
- How should I conduct my life?

As children we all ask these fundamental questions, but as we get
older we often try to ignore them because they seem just too big to
answer, or else we look for the solutions in religion, philosophy or
science. As limited human beings, we cannot expect to grasp the
answers easily, even if they exist.

Wise people in all epochs have advised people to look within
themselves for understanding – as we change and grow, so will our
insight into the nature of things.

By becoming a medium you are setting out on a rather special and
unknown road, so make sure you have sincere intentions. I hope
that this book will help you to get started on this strange and
wonderful journey.

I should like to thank Mike Jay, Dr Edward Featherstone,
Christopher Titmuss, Richard Craze, Carol Skoniecki, Dennis Peat,
Tim Hunt and Dilys Guildford for the valuable help and advice they
gave me during the writing of this book. The opinions expressed in
this book are mine, not theirs.

ᴆo spirits really exist?

Where did you come from, baby dear?
Out of the everywhere and into here.

George MacDonald, *At the Back of the North Wind*

As you are reading this book, you probably feel that spirits do exist – but you live in a world where the dominant belief is that they don't. So how can we make sense of these opposing opinions? The main argument of the rationalist, scientific view of the world is that one can't measure spirits or other supernatural phenomena in the same way that one can measure things that exist in the three dimensional world. There is therefore no satisfactory evidence for their existence.

Many mediums seek evidence to satisfy the scientists, and you often hear statements such as, 'the existence of auras is now proven', or 'the activities of spirits are measurable with scientific instruments'.

Unfortunately, this is not true. The fact is that despite attempts over several centuries to reconcile science with esoteric lore, they remain resolutely at odds. In my opinion, there really isn't any point in trying to do so, especially if, like most people, you didn't study science beyond your mid-teens.

Quantum physics

This is not to say that scientific theories about the world don't change – they do, and there is a large field of popular literature that attempts to show correspondences between ancient ideas about the world and current scientific thinking in many fields. Books like *The Tao of Physics* and *The Dancing WuLi Masters* (*see* Further Reading) argue that ancient oriental descriptions of the universe are similar to, or are allegories of, modern discoveries in quantum physics. The trouble with quantum physics is that the ultrasubatomic processes that it studies are so malleable and strange that it is possible to extrapolate from them in almost any direction – so unless you really understand the mathematics, it is useless to try to make quantum physics fit esoteric ideas about the world.

Near death experiences

We shouldn't feel the need to search through popular scientific literature for absolute proofs of our inner experiences; people who do so are invariably selective, picking up on the work that appears to support their ideas, and ignoring that which doesn't. On the whole, it is unrealistic to try to make science fit esoteric ideas.

If, however, you are interested in a general way in what science has to say about inner experience, it is worth reading about the research being done on the brain. Sue Blackmore, for example, of the Brain and Perception unit at Bristol University in the UK, has written two interesting books, *Adventures of a Parapsychologist* and *Dying to Live* (*see* Further Reading), which are sober and honest accounts of her explorations in this area. Dr Blackmore looks at a lot of accounts of near death experiences and has identified different levels of such experiences. She looks at the people who reach the 'furthest levels', so to speak, asks why that is, and questions people about their feelings when they return from apparent death. She points out that there are a lot of neurological events which happen

during the near death experience which account for some of the things that people report happening; for example, as the brain gets starved of oxygen there is a 'cortical shutdown' which has the effect of making the edges of a person's vision go black, with a bright light appearing at the centre.

Dr Blackmore notes that many people return from near death experiences feeling that they have changed for the better. She thinks that the reason for this is that the 'ego' dissolves during dying – and that if a person is revived, he or she somehow realises that the ego is a kind of illusion over which we have some control. On their return people can reassess themselves, let go of what is not important in their personalities and retain what matters.

Kirlian photography and aura goggles

You may have seen Kirlian photographs of living things, such as hands and leaves, which seem to show a kind of aura around them. These photographs are produced by generating a high-frequency electric field (very high voltage and low amperage) which has a marked tendency to travel on the surfaces of things and not to penetrate them. What it seems to do is to outline some subtle field of energy that surrounds living things – what the Russians call 'bioplasma'. Is it anything to do with the aura that mediums and clairvoyants speak of? No one knows – yet!

We will look in detail at methods for developing your sensitivity to auras later. Sometimes people use 'aura goggles' to do this. Aura goggles were discovered by a Dr Kilner in the 1930s; they consist of a 'dye cyanin', olive-green crystals with a metallic sheen, which are placed between glass and act as an optical filter for visualising infrared radiations and magnetic fields. What you see is one intense border around an object, with two other less distinct borders slightly further out. So is this the aura, or a facet of it? Science doesn't know.

Is reality culturally based?

It should be clear by now that the science is fragmentary, offering us tantalising glimpses of a possible future reconciliation between spiritual and scientific views of the world. What we should realise is that it is not good science to explain away things which you don't understand – a good scientist tries to investigate what he or she doesn't understand, not just to dismiss it. Nevertheless, there are many arrogant sceptics who overstep scientific competence by categorically dismissing the experiences of mediums. They do this, I believe, not because of their scientific training, but because they are steeped in modern culture in which there is no room for the belief in spirits.

There is no doubt that we, in modern developed countries, live in a culture where the existence of a spirit world is not generally accepted. It also happens to be the dominant culture on earth at this time – and people in dominant cultures can always argue that the fact that they are dominant proves that they are completely right in their ideas about the world. However, ours is exceptional in its rejection of the existence of spirits; most cultures throughout history have nurtured a belief in them. Even today, there are many places where almost everyone believes in spirits, and it is the rational, materialistic sceptic who is in the minority.

Let's look at two of the 'alternative realities' currently competing with our own.

The Inuit

The Inuit, or Eskimos, of the Arctic have daily and intimate contact with spiritual forces. Amongst the Ihalmiut, an inland tribe, valuable *Irinjelo*, or spirit songs, are passed secretly from parents to their children. These Irinjelo are used to cure particular illnesses which, the Ihalmiut believe, are caused by spirits. Here's the story of how an Irinjelo was used on a Canadian explorer, Farley Mowat:

On one of my trips with Ootek out to the Barrens, I developed severe cramps in my stomach and became deathly sick. I was afraid of appendicitis, but there was nothing I could do to help myself except lie quietly in my tent and try not to groan with pain. Ootek was concerned. He brought me hot tea every few minutes and constantly inquired how I was feeling. Yet he seemed preoccupied and shy. It was only after some hours of indecision that Ootek could finally bring himself to speak of a point which was bothering him. Then, very tentatively, he asked me if he could try one of his own personal Irinjelo for stomach ailments on me. He had hesitated because he was afraid I would scorn his offer – being a white man and therefore a master of superior charms. Actually I had no faith in his charm, but I did not wish to repulse his kindness, and so I told him that I would be grateful.

He took a tin cup filled with fresh water and, holding it carefully in front of him, began to walk slowly around the outside of the tent where I lay. As he walked, he sang his Irinjelo, a monotonous dirge in a minor key. At intervals he ceased singing and addressed himself to the cup of water, urging the evil to leave me and the good to come in. All this was continued for perhaps five or ten minutes. Then Ootek returned to the tent, gave me the water and told me to swallow it down.

Though I was sick, I could see that he was almost abjectly afraid that I would laugh, or toss the water away. He wanted very greatly to help me, but he was also deeply afraid that he was exposing both himself and his beliefs to my ridicule.

Well, I took the water, with all proper solemnity, drank it, and was at once seized with a violent urge to urinate. I barely got out of the tent in time and the urine was so hot and painful I was almost convinced Ootek had added some irritant to the water. Still, I had not seen him do it, and anyway I could not understand how any irritant could have functioned so quickly.

While I was engrossed in this problem, and with the burning pain in my loins, it suddenly dawned on me that my belly pains had vanished. Ootek was standing, watching me from the door,

7

with a strained smile on his face. I gave him an answering grin, and he promptly beamed like an idiot and rushed off to cook me some supper.

I suppose it was just a happy coincidence – for it was certainly not faith that cured me ... not mine, at any rate. When I thanked Ootek for his aid, I also asked him what had happened and he replied with beautiful simplicity that the good had come in with the water, and that the bad had gone out with the water!

(From *People of the Deer* by Farley Mowat, Little, Brown and Company, 1952.)

Umbanda, Voodoo and Candomblé

These are hybrid religions which have developed out of the suffering of millions of West Africans who were taken as slaves to the Americas. They are rooted in the ancient religious beliefs of West African tribes, but have incorporated many new elements. Called *Voodoo* in Haiti, *Shango* in Trinidad, *Santeria* in Cuba, *Obeayisne* in Jamaica, and *Umbanda* and *Candomblé* in Brazil, these new religions are vibrant and evolving.

Central to these religions are the non–human spirits known as *lwa* in Haiti and *orixas* in Brazil; they are beings of great power which can harm or help the living, depending on how they are treated. *Houngans,* or priests, help people to understand the activities of the lwa. The lwa have favourites amongst the living, and each person has particular lwa with whom they are spiritually associated. The lwa can possess human beings, and often do this, both during religious ceremonies, and spontaneously during daily life.

If you haven't seen this for yourself, it is hard to appreciate just how real these forces are. I have watched respectable Brazilian women become possessed by 'Madame Pomba Gira' (Spinning Dove), and start behaving wildly, gulping down alcohol, laughing and swearing, behaving seductively and dancing until they dropped. Pomba Gira is a kind of goddess of sex and violence – earthy and uncontrollable, she imbues her followers with superhuman strength. Three strong men cannot hold down a woman possessed by Pomba Gira.

8

Figure 1.1 The 'seal' of Pomba Gira

Stories like this give these religions a bad reputation. Such beings are not evil, though; they are seen as forces which, with the help of the houngan, can be channelled for good. Not all of them behave so dramatically; 'Preto Velho' (Old Black) is the once-human spirit of a slave who is full of wisdom and good advice.

Figure 1.2 Preto Velho, the wise guide

For their devotees, these spirits provide a comprehensive system for living their lives and relating to the things seen and unseen.

Comparing Beliefs

So what are we to make of all these strange ideas? Who is right? Well, it doesn't really work like that. The point is that there are many, many other ways of looking at the world than our generally gloomy, aggressive 'modern' view. If we are right about everything, why aren't we always happy? One of the most noticeable features of what used to be called primitive peoples is that they are so open, so pleasant, so great-hearted, so alive to the world – when we don't interfere, at least. Their beliefs are well adapted to their ways of life – and notably ill adapted to the modern world, as is evident in the tragic condition of the indigenous peoples all over the globe who are being forced to give up their ancient ways.

Belief systems are constantly changing. You only have to think back a few years to see how fast, and how radically this can happen. Back in the 1950s people had enormous confidence in the use of chemicals in agriculture, for instance; today, everyone is terrified of poisoning the earth. Think of your own parents and grandparents – didn't they have ideas about the world that seem completely wrong to you?

Many people these days think that it doesn't really matter what you believe – it's all relative, they say, and one person's reality is just as good as another's. This can lead to a state of mind where nothing seems very real at all and every idea becomes equally meaningless. This is a very pusillanimous condition which doesn't get you anywhere. To develop as human beings, we need, at least, to have a working hypothesis about the world.

Only the spiritually blind think that there are no mysteries. And only the arrogant think that they understand everything. So for now, let's simply accept that the majority of cultures throughout the history of the human race have had the idea that there are sentient beings out there, some of which used to have a human body, and some that didn't.

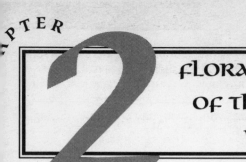

FLORA AND FAUNA OF THE UNSEEN WORLD

I can call spirits from the vasty deep.

Why, so can I, or so can any man.
But will they come when you do call for them?

Shakespeare, *Henry IV Part 1*

In Chapter 1 we looked at the variety of human belief; from now on, we will stop talking about beliefs, and concentrate on descriptions of the spirit world or worlds. To develop as a medium, you need to put aside your rational mind for a while in order to develop your capacity to sense what cannot be experienced in your normal, everyday state of mind.

FORMS OF SPIRIT

Spirits come in many forms. In this chapter we will look at this vast array; I find it useful to use the analogy of the natural world – just as there is a rich diversity of plants, animals, and minerals in the natural world, so it is in the spiritual world, only more so. Even a spiritual 'fungus' has its place, but one wouldn't expect it to be able to do much.

Spirits have many names and are divided into many categories, according to the different traditions. Terminology can be contentious; many groups use different words to mean the same

11

thing, and the same word to mean different things. Don't get hung up on the names; it is more important to try to understand what is being described, and see how it relates to your own experience. The descriptions in this chapter are not intended to be comprehensive – there are other entities and forms which you may encounter during your travels within yourself.

Spirits of the Dead

These are the spirits that most people think of first. Just as there are wise and foolish people amongst the living, so it is with the dead. The dead are undergoing transformations, as the living are, and are definitely not omniscient or perfect. Many schools of mediumship concentrate exclusively on contacting the spirits of dead people.

Footprints and Shells

Go to a house where someone has recently died, and you can often sense that something of them still remains. This is not the soul of the person, but a kind of psychic 'footprint' which they have left behind, which gradually disappears as time passes.

Many hauntings continue long after a person has died – sometimes for centuries afterwards. I think of these as 'shells', similar to footprints, but containing more power. It is easy to mistake such a shell for the person who created it – if you see, say, a white lady who always passes along a corridor at a certain time, or you hear the tramp of boots where once a long-dead troop of soldiers marched, you are probably not sensing spirits of the dead, but energy forms which they created when they were still living, and which have carried on, like ripples in water after a stone has fallen into a pond.

These energy forms may be disturbing, but they are not really dangerous, and are best left alone – they are not sentient, and certainly cannot communicate with people in any meaningful sense. If they become disturbing to the living they can be dispelled by exorcism or other purification techniques.

Larvae

Sometimes you can see, with your spiritual vision, energy forms like coloured blobs floating around which can attach themselves to a person's psychic body. With cleansing, they can be removed. These 'larvae' are created from dark desires within one person, before floating off and bothering others of like mind.

Spirits related to nature

Folklore everywhere has tales of these beings – pixies, fairies, elves, trolls, nymphs, dryads, fauns, and little people are just a few of the names given to this type of being. They are sentient, but shy of humans. Animals are aware of them, and children can sometimes see them. Their main task seems to be related to processes in nature and they are generally tied to particular places. People who work on the land and are close to nature are often aware of them, and take great trouble not to upset them – all across the world we find taboos against cutting down certain plants, or interfering with certain spots, for fear of disturbing these spirits. Ruling over the nature spirits are 'elemental kings', which have greater power.

The work of the Findhorn Foundation in Scotland (*see* Useful Addresses) is related to these beings. By contacting them, the people at Findhorn have been able to produce plants of extraordinary size and fruitfulness.

Unruly spirits

By 'unruly spirits' I mean non-human forces which occasionally wreak havoc, such as poltergeists which throw crockery and turn over chairs. Like nature spirits, to whom they are related, they are generally tied to places, and they seem to need a living person who is psychically open in order to manifest. Poltergeist activity, for instance, is sometimes associated with a disturbed teenager living in the house.

There is a kind of magic which seeks to command and control these forces in order to obtain material benefits. Don't be tempted to practise it – you be may be successful, and if you are, you will surely end up wishing you hadn't been.

ANGELS

Many non-human entities may be called 'angels', but really fall into the other categories described in this chapter.

Imagine an entity so large that to attract its attention is as useless as a bacterium trying to attract the attention of a human being.

To get an idea of such a being, take a minute to contemplate the vastness of space. Here we are, the dominant life form on the third planet of an average star in a backwater of an average galaxy, thinking that we are the most important things in the universe. Now imagine another part of the universe, so far away that even if we travelled for millions of years at the speed of light we wouldn't reach it. At that place, picture a nebula, say – a gigantic cloud of coloured gases and particles of extraordinary beauty, of such size that a thousand solar systems would only be a pinprick on its edge. Perhaps you can see a picture in it – a face, say, or a building, or an animal. Now imagine the spirit of this nebula, rippling, throbbing, making music that will last aeons. What could a being of such size, and so far away, have to do with such tiny, short-lived creatures as us?

Tradition says that there are angels who have specific jobs to do with the spiritual development of human beings, and who, therefore, do sometimes make contact. In Chapter 5 on channelling we will examine these in more detail.

DEVILS

Traditions tell us of a whole hierarchy of angelic beings who are 'fallen'. They may have great beauty and power, but they are not good – they tempt us and lead us astray. As long as our hearts are pure they cannot harm us, but if we take a step towards them, they

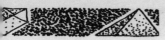

will take great leaps and bounds towards us, feeding on our fears and weaknesses. The legendary pact that Doctor Faustus made with the devil has a psychological reality – our desires and ambitions can lead us down very dark roads. A wise medium does not toy with these forces.

The fallen angels encourage us to get inflated ideas about ourselves; in mythic terms, these angels beget with men a race of giants who eventually attempt to devour the human race. They promulgate the lie that there is nothing more important than humankind and its achievements.

Gods

Throughout history many people have worshipped entities which, though divine, are nevertheless created beings. The great spiritual discoveries of monotheism have taught us that we do not need their intercession to have direct and real contact with the ultimate cause of things – what is called the one God. The lesser gods are still worshipped on earth, notably in the surviving 'pagan' religions of Hinduism, Umbanda and Voodoo.

Buddhism tends to regard these lesser gods as beings which, though highly evolved, are still subject to cravings which will ultimately lead to their death and rebirth in lesser forms. Christianity, Islam and Judaism, on the other hand, take the view that they are false gods whom it is wrong to worship, and generally give them a bad press, which is not surprising since these three versions of monotheism all developed in environments where the worship of pagan gods was creating a lot of evil – the angry gods of the Middle East who demanded human sacrifice and the corrupting gods of the later Roman world were doing nothing to help their devotees become better people.

These are subtle matters; if you look deeply enough into paganism you find monotheism within it. I do not regard the worship of lesser gods as necessarily, or essentially, evil. They can be true paths for sincere devotees.

As an unbeliever, can you sense these entities? Undoubtedly – go to India, and feel the presence of the goddess Kali brooding over her sacred city, Calcutta, or to Egypt to feel Horus still hovering about the pyramids, centuries after its devotees have gone.

Zeitgeists and big-idea spirits

Zeitgeist is a German word meaning 'the spirit of the times'. In the first half of the twentieth century, the zeitgeist was very much one of a desperate search for a new kind of social order to replace the autocracies of the past. The desperate conflict between communism and fascism can be seen as a reflection of this – both ideologies sought to provide a new way of life which was going to make things fairer for everyone, and to remove the power from what both sides saw as the tyrannies of capitalists, landowners and hereditary ruling castes.

It is possible to contact zeitgeists, of other times as well as that of our own. They are not conscious entities exactly – more like a principle, or a force, which expresses a view of the world held by a large group of people. They can manifest in your spiritual vision in symbolic form, and are often pictured in art. What I call 'big-idea' spirits are similar – they are the spirits of the big ideas that move people at particular times, such as today's Green movement.

In Spain, there is a monument to the dead of the Civil War (Valle de los Caidos), some kilometres from Madrid. It is an awe-inspiring place – as you drive to it, all you see is a massive cross 150 metres (492 ft) high on top of a mountain. You clamber up massive steps to the entrance into the mountain. Inside, huge angels in black stone glower down on you, leaning on their swords. Walking down a long corridor into the heart of the mountain, you eventually enter a church. A hole in the roof of this church reaches up to the cross outside, and at certain times a shaft of light shines down upon the altar. Beneath the altar is buried the corpse of General Franco, the Spanish dictator. I often wonder how many of the thousands of foreign tourists who go there each year realise that this monument was built by forced labour after the Civil War – hundreds of

anarchist prisoners died as they hewed out the rock. For me, this is no place for true worship, but a temple to the spirit of fascism, a devilish entity who tempts humans with visions of attaining superhuman power by force and cruelty to others.

Why do some religions forbid contact with spirits?

Christianity, Judaism and Islam recognise the existence of spirits, but expressly forbid contact with them, yet their holy books are full of stories of angels and other entities having commerce with living people. Looking more closely at these religions we find that they all allow qualified specialists, be they priests, rabbis, marabouts or sheikhs, to have dealings with spirits, albeit in a rigorous and limited way. Mediumship is generally forbidden to laypeople. If you take a cynical view, you might say that they forbid mediumship only because it interferes with their own monopoly on spiritual life, and while there is some truth in this, it is not the whole story. A more charitable view is that most people are not spiritually evolved enough to get much real benefit from contact with spirits, and that these religions want to emphasise the point that we don't need to have any contact with spirits in order to develop.

In New Age thinking, it is argued that we are entering an era when many people are ready for knowledge of the spirit worlds, and that the time is ripe for us to investigate them.

The importance of protection

Some people reading this book will have already had disturbing contacts with spirits, perhaps during the use of psychedelic drugs. If

you are one of these, I have an important message for you: Don't worry! You need to develop balance and harmony within yourself, and this will take time. Don't rush about telling worldly people about your experiences, or you may end up in a mental hospital – find a wise, good-hearted person to help you heal the rents in your psyche. If your need is real, such a person will definitely appear. It doesn't matter what you've seen, or what you have done – there is hope.

A wicked old monk used to tell me that contacting spirits is like a road that slopes downhill gently at first, and then suddenly opens up into a chasm which you can't climb out of. He wanted to frighten people away from genuine spiritual enquiry. If you are sincere and grounded, you have nothing to fear from your investigations into these matters.

When you open up your psyche it is like a beacon lighting up in the spirit worlds – all kinds of entities will start to take an interest in you, and, as we have seen from the descriptions above, many of these entities do not have your best interests at heart, to put it mildly. It is important to develop in such a way as to banish the bad spirits and align yourself with the good ones. To achieve this, you need to develop your ability to protect yourself.

PRACTICE

SPIRITUAL PROTECTION

Protection is essential for mediumship. You need to let yourself and the spirit world know that you are firmly on the side of Good. Protection exercises have the effect of warding off negative energies which might otherwise cause mischief.

You must choose a symbol; it can be any image you are able to picture mentally. Traditionally, people choose a symbol from the religion in which they were brought up. This is because even if you are no longer committed to that religion, the image represents ideas which are deeply embedded in your psyche. Using the Cross, the Star of David or the Buddha helps many people to focus on feelings of goodness and purity. If you don't

feel comfortable with a traditional religious image, then choose something less conventional – what's important is that you sincerely feel that the image represents the principles of goodness and purity.

For the sake of this exercise we will use the Cross, the most important symbol of the Christian faith, but you can use any symbol you wish.

1   Sit naturally in a straight-backed chair with your hands on your knees, and close your eyes. Close your mouth and breathe through your nose.

2   Mentally check your position. Straighten your spine and relax your shoulders.

3   Move your awareness to the top of your head and, as slowly as you can, move your attention down your body, relaxing each part as you go.

4   Become aware of your breathing. Let it flow in and out of your nose naturally.

5   Become aware of your state of mind. How are you feeling? Are you edgy, angry, or worried?

6   Return your attention to your breathing and relax.

7   Mentally picture the Cross in front of you. Picture its size, colour and shape. Think of a white light surrounding it, radiating Love, Wisdom and Compassion.

8   Remind yourself that nothing can hurt you, since you are bathed in the pure light of the Cross.

9   Resolve to dedicate yourself to doing good, to yourself and to others.

10 Slowly open your eyes.

Practise this exercise for a few minutes every day. After a few weeks you will find that it becomes much easier to recall the symbol clearly whenever you wish. Use the symbol as a 'psychic anchor'; if you ever become disturbed or frightened when working as a medium, recall the symbol and use it to drive off negative forces.

3 the power of silence

..the sole purpose of human existence is to kindle a light in the darkness of mere being.

Carl Jung

You cannot perform any spiritual or psychic practice properly without developing an inner stillness; it is the single most important quality for becoming sensitive to the subtle worlds.

After you have finished reading this paragraph, stop what you are doing and listen. What do you hear? There may be a prominent sound – listen to it for a few moments and then see if you can hear others. Try to distinguish between all the different sounds that you hear, where they are coming from and what is causing them.

The skill of being still

If you want to become a medium you probably already have some skill at being still. You need to develop it: spend part of every day alone and in silence.

The barriers to being still can be divided into two – barriers that are outside you in the environment, and barriers that are inside your own mind, body and spirit. By learning to recognise what is causing a disturbance you can find ways to be silent even in the most difficult circumstances.

External Disturbances

In the beginning, the noise of radios, TVs and cars can be very disturbing. If you live somewhere which is noisy, you need to seek out a quiet place where you can go each day to be silent. Even in a big city you can find quiet places, such as:

- parks
- libraries
- museums and art galleries
- places of worship

Find a place that suits you and try to go there every day.

Another source of disturbance is bad air. If you are sitting somewhere which has a strong chemical smell, or is very dusty, smoky or stale, your breathing will be affected and your mind will be disturbed. Sniff the air before you sit.

People can be the worst disturbance of all, especially if you are behaving unusually. If your nearest and dearest won't leave you alone when you are trying to be silent, don't make a big issue out of it – just find ways of incorporating quiet times into your daily routine. For instance, if you go shopping alone, you can stop at a park for a while on the way.

Everyone needs to be alone and quiet for part of the day. Look at your own life – if it doesn't have any space for quietness, you need to change your habits.

Internal Disturbances

Here are some common types:

Physical   If you are tired, nervous, ill, drunk, have just eaten a heavy meal or chain-smoked twenty cigarettes you will not be able to be still and in a proper state of mind. Try sitting first thing in the morning, when your body is fresh. You will find that your body behaves differently at different times of the day; it is said that the

best time for practising silence is between 2a.m. and 5a.m., when the world is asleep and subtle energies abound. Once you have established the habit of sitting in silence, experiment by doing it at different times of the day, and observe the changes your body undergoes during the twenty-four-hour cycle.

Mental   Your mind and body are intimately connected, and when one is disturbed the other is also affected. A common mental disturbance is to experience a torrent of angry, worried, fearful or vengeful thoughts. Often people try to suppress these, or ignore them, but I am suggesting that you adopt the following attitude:

'Negative' thoughts and feelings are perfectly natural to the human mind. If you think of them as being tensions, or toxins, within you, then you can see that it is better to let them out than to keep them bottled up and festering inside. By giving these thoughts and feelings free passage through your mind they gradually lose their power and disappear. This is a cleansing process, and is one of the most important reasons for practising silence.

The same principle applies to other types of mental disturbance; for instance, you may be strongly affected by recurring fantasies. Let them pass through your mind – if they appear, it means that your mind is using them to develop itself, so don't worry about what they may mean. As with dreams, fantasies are a necessary part of mental life.

Spiritual   Perhaps this is an artificial category; after all, where does the mind end and the spirit begin? The kind of disturbances that I tend to think of as 'spiritual' are those that go very deep – the kind of impulse that wakes you up in the middle of the night, thinking 'Why I am I here?', for instance, or a recurring feeling of regret or guilt that goes back to your childhood. They are thoughts and feelings within you that go back a long way and have influenced you greatly – quite unlike the 'Did I remember to turn the water heater off?' type of ephemeral mental disturbance. When spiritual disturbances appear in your mind, just watch them and let them go – eventually, they will be resolved.

PRACTICE

SITTING IN SILENCE

This seems a simple exercise, but it is very powerful. Go to your quiet place and sit down – either cross-legged on a cushion on the floor, or, if this is too uncomfortable, on a straight-backed chair. Close your mouth and breathe through your nostrils. Sit up tall in a firm, comfortable posture. Check that your spine is straight and that you are balanced. Now close your eyes and start to relax your body. Start at the top of your head and move downwards, relaxing your head, neck, shoulders, arms, chest, abdomen, legs and feet.

Figure 3.1 Sitting in silence

Now check your whole body for any remaining tensions, and relax them.

Become aware of your breath moving in and out of your nostrils. Focus on the point where the breath is entering and leaving your body, and just watch. Thoughts and feelings may appear in your mind – let them pass freely, and keep returning your attention on the breath.

After a while, open your eyes and end your sitting. At first you may find it difficult to sit for more than a few minutes, but with practice you can learn to sit for long periods. Try to practise every day.

The technique described above is a powerful cleanser. It is not a method for contacting spirits (we'll look at exercises for this later), so don't try to combine it with other practices – for example, if you start seeing visions, don't get involved with them, but let them pass, as you would any other mental disturbance. The object of the exercise is not to see visions, attain enlightenment, get magical powers or anything else; the object is simply to learn how to be still. After a period of regular practice, you will start to see benefits from it in your daily life, but don't get excited about them – just keep up the practice!

RelaxatioN

Many of us need to learn to relax, and although the sitting technique described above will help, there may be times when you are just too tense to practise. For this reason, it is useful to train yourself in specific relaxation methods. The following method, the 'psychic sleep', is very powerful, and, as we will see, can be refined to the point where it can be used in specific kinds of mediumship.

PRACTICE

Relaxation exercise (preliminary to the psychic sleep)

Lie flat on your back on the floor, with your feet apart and your arms away from your body, the palms of your hands facing upwards.

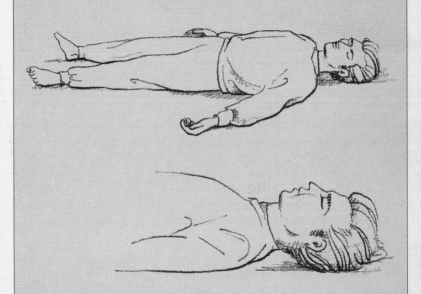

Figure 3.2 Relaxation

Lift up your head for a moment and check that your body is balanced and straight, with each leg and arm the same distance away from your body as the one on the other side. Put your head

back, and check that there is no tension in your neck and that you can swallow easily. From now on, try not to move until the end of the practice.

Become aware of the pains and tensions in your body. Where are they? Try to identify where they are coming from.

Calm yourself, and breathe naturally through your nostrils. Be aware that if you focus on any particular part of your body, more blood will flow there, nourishing and healing it.

Now move your attention to the big toe on your right foot. Picture it in your mind, and feel it relaxing. Then move your attention to the whole of your right foot – try to feel all the little bones, tendons and joints in your right foot, and deeply relax them.

Now move your attention to the lower part of your right leg – deeply relax your calf and shin.

Focus on your right knee, and deeply relax it – right inside the joint.

Focus on your right thigh and hip, and deeply relax them.

Now become aware of the whole of your right leg and foot. Let all the remaining tensions go, and feel it tingling with warm, healing energy.

Move your attention to the big toe of your left foot, and repeat the whole process for the left foot and leg.

Become aware of both your legs and feel as if they are melting into a warm sea of healthy, healing energy.

Now become aware of your bowels and genitalia. Feel them relaxing and healing. Relax your buttocks and stomach. Then move your attention to your chest, and deeply relax your heart. Focus on the base of your spine at the back, and move your awareness up the spine, relaxing each vertebra as you go, as far as the base of your neck. Become aware of your whole

torso, and feel it melting and relaxing into a sea of warm, healing energy.

Move your attention to the fingers of your right hand, and relax them. Relax your right wrist, your right forearm, elbow and upper arm. Become aware of the whole arm and hand and relax it – feel it grow warm and tingling. Now repeat the process with your left hand and arm.

Deeply relax your shoulders. then relax your neck, your jaw, your lips and your tongue. Relax all the muscles in your face, around your ears, eyes and eyebrows. Relax your forehead and all the muscles around your scalp. Deeply relax the top of your head.

Feel your whole body relaxed, warm and tingling. Look for any remaining tensions, and relax them. Feel energised and harmonised.

Now slowly move your fingers, raise your hands and touch your face. Slowly sit up and open your eyes. It is important to end the relaxation slowly – if you jump up quickly, you will lose many of the benefits.

Notes on Relaxation

With regular practice you can obtain very deep states of relaxation with the above technique. Don't do it for too long at first – about ten minutes is plenty for beginners, and you will lessen the benefit by extending the time until you are more proficient.

People often find that their bodies twitch and jerk during the exercise. This is not abnormal – just learn from your body how to release the tensions that cause the twitching.

Sometimes you may suddenly find yourself outside of your body, looking down on it. This is nothing to worry about – you will return, probably with a sudden thump!

Try not to let yourself fall asleep during the exercise. You are training yourself to retain your awareness in rarefied states, and falling asleep is a way of avoiding this. You can use the technique in order to help you fall asleep at night, however.

PRACTICE

The psychic sleep

Once you have become proficient at relaxing, you can deepen the experience greatly. Instead of ending the session at the point described in the exercise above, concentrate on the top of your head.

Imagine waves of relaxing energy entering the top of your head and rippling down through your body. Each time you breathe in, imagine another wave of bright, healing energy entering the top of your head and rippling downwards. Each time you breathe out, imagine the energy rippling down through the whole of your body and out of your feet, taking with it all your remaining tensions.

Feel your whole body melting into a vast ocean of energy, as if it is ice melting into a sea of warm water. Experience this for several minutes.

Now concentrate on your heart. Picture warm, vibrant energy issuing from your heart and travelling to your legs. Feel your legs and feet tingling with the energy. Then feel the energy returning to your heart.

Send energy from your heart out to your chest and abdomen. Then feel it returning to your heart.

Send energy from your heart out to your arms and hands. Feel them tingle as the energy reaches them. Then send the energy back to your heart.

Send energy from your heart to your head. Feel your head becoming light and full of energy. Then send the energy back to your heart.

Now send energy from your heart to your whole body – feel your whole body tingling with energy. Send the energy back from your body to your heart.

Now send energy from your heart out to cover the whole world. Feel it returning from all parts of the world to your heart.

Send energy from your heart out to the planets and the sun, and then feel it returning to your heart.

Send energy out from your heart to the whole universe – feel the whole universe glowing and pulsing with positive, warm life energy. Imagine that you are the whole universe – as if the universe is within you. Now feel the energy returning from all parts of the universe to your heart.

If any parts of your body are in need of healing, you can now concentrate on them, sending healing energy to them to recharge and energise them. Feel confident that you are becoming healed and energised.

To outside observers, your body will appear to be asleep – but to you, it is they who may appear to be asleep. With practice, you can direct your psychic energy at will for many purposes in this state; for example, to read the 'Akashic Records', as Edgar Cayce did (*see* page 48).

When it is time to end the session, become aware of your physical body. This is a good time to make positive resolutions and affirmations – in this deep state, any strong suggestions you make to yourself (e.g. 'I will give up smoking') will take root.

Now very gradually move your fingers, raise your hands and touch your face. Very slowly sit up and open your eyes.

NOTES ON THE PSYCHIC SLEEP

The theory of this technique is that you are teaching yourself to liberate your psychic energy from total identification with the

physical body. The idea is that normally we hold a kind of unconscious picture of our bodies in our heads which absorbs our energies; this practice enables us to expand ourselves beyond our normal limitations.

Naturally, this begs a lot of questions, such as 'What is this "energy" we are dealing with?' In Chapter 4 we will look at some of the traditional explanations for these phenomena – but if you only know the theory, it will be of no use to you, so practise these exercises, and experience the effects for yourself.

Ground rules for mediumship

All spiritual traditions emphasise the importance of proper discipline when you are training. If you don't discipline yourself, you will not be able to make progress in a healthy and balanced way. Here are a few basic rules to follow:

1 **Be non-violent.** This is similar to the first of the Ten Commandments, 'Thou shalt not kill'. It doesn't just mean that you should avoid physical violence, but also that you must try to avoid speaking and thinking violently. Even telling someone to 'drop dead' in jest counts as violence. Avoid being spiteful and manipulative, and remember to be kind to yourself, too – dosing yourself with unnecessary medicines, for instance, is a form of violence.

2 **Be honest.** Tell the truth, and be truthful to yourself. Dishonesty prevents your mind from being clear, and attracts negative forces to you. This doesn't mean that you have to trust everyone – we live in a very dishonest world, after all. Truthfulness implies objectivity and realism; check your facts, and don't take everything you see and hear at face value. Try to strike a balance between cynicism and gullibility, and develop your ability to discriminate between truth and falsehood.

3 **Don't steal.** This applies as much to intangibles, such as taking the credit for someone else's work, as it does to stealing objects.
4 **Don't be avaricious.** This doesn't mean that you mustn't make any money, or acquire good things, but rather that 'enough is as good as a feast'. The endless effort to amass more and more money, or to become more and more famous, does you no good at all.
5 **Be balanced about sex.** Sex can enslave people, absorbing all their spare psychic energy.
6 **Be clean.** This means you should keep your house, your clothes and your body clean, that you should eat clean food (see below), and also that you should try to have a clean mind, by not filling it with rubbish. Mental cleanliness can be difficult, and we will look at ways of staying mentally clean throughout this book. Here's a simple step you can take, though – watch less TV!
7 **Be content.** By all means have ambitions, but don't let thoughts about the future, or the past, prevent you from enjoying the present. Nothing lasts forever, so appreciate what life offers you as you move through it.
8 **Be attentive.** Cultivate an awareness of what is going on within you and without you.
9 **Learn useful things.** Develop your skills and understanding in all spheres of life open to you.
10 **Surrender your little self to the universe.** As individuals we are limited, but inside each of us is a spark of divinity.

These rules are not designed to turn you into a sanctimonious 'creeping Jesus' who revels in a phony piety, but are actually very practical guidelines which will help you to develop spiritually.

Diet

The industrialisation of the world has affected our food; there is much more of it than there has ever been, but much of it is processed and treated in ways that spoil it. Modern life has made us

neurotic about our diets, and the media constantly throws up new food scares. Relax! Your body knows what is good food, so learn to listen to it.

It is up to you whether you want to become a vegetarian. In general, it is a good idea not to eat meat more than once or twice a week, and to avoid processed foods and stimulants such as tea and coffee. Fresh local produce is generally the best source of nourishment. As you develop as a medium, you may decide to follow stricter dietary regimes; when you are ready to do so, you will get a sign.

Some people drive themselves crazy trying to follow difficult diets; this is unnecessary. If you are an active, productive person there will inevitably be times when the only food available is not particularly wholesome. At such times, don't make a fuss – just eat what you need.

Clean water is very important. Drink at least two pints of water a day. In cities, the water is usually unwholesome, so try to drink genuine mineral water – you can buy it cheaply wholesale in large containers.

Taking stock of yourself

Now that you have read this chapter, sit down and practise the sitting in silence exercise. Afterwards, think about why you are interested in mediumship; what is it in you that attracts you to it? Take stock of yourself – how many of the ground rules do you already practise? What is stopping you from practising the others, and how can you overcome these obstacles?

4

TYPES OF
MEDIUMSHIP AND
THEIR USES

*Our normal waking consciousness, rational
consciousness as we call it, is but one special type
of consciousness, whilst all about it, parted from it
by the filmiest of screens, there lie potential forms
of consciousness entirely different ... No account of
the universe in its totality can be final which leaves
these other forms of consciousness quite
disregarded.*

William James, *The Varieties of Religious Experience*, Longman, 1902

Anyone who can feel the influence of spirits, however faintly, can be called a medium. It seems that this ability, or collection of abilities, is natural in human beings, and one can say that almost everybody is a potential medium. Usually, though, we call mediums people who have quite a high degree of mediumistic ability.

To become aware of unseen worlds, we need to get out of our everyday, busy states of mind. Figure 4.1 illustrates one way of explaining why this is.

Together, the boat and the diving capsule represent a human being; the boat represents the 'higher self', meaning that deep part of us which is concerned with spiritual things, and the diving capsule represents the 'lower self', meaning the part of us which is concerned with material things. The capsule itself represents the physical body. Inside it is a little person who you can think of as the personality, or ego – it is the part of yourself that you normally think

Figure 4.1 The higher and lower selves

of as 'me'. The ego is looking out at a small area of the sea bed which is lit by the light of its awareness. The ego doesn't see any of the other things in the picture, such as the sea creatures, which represent disembodied beings.

Up above, the captain of the boat has a broader view of what is going on. He waits patiently for the diver down below to complete his mission.

This is a crude analogy, perhaps, but it may help you to appreciate the essential point about mediumistic practice; the everyday 'you' grubs about on the sea bed of daily life, unaware of what it can't see. In order to become aware of 'hidden' things, the little everyday 'you' has to train itself to expand its awareness. This is done by practising exercises such as were introduced in Chapter 3. Don't expect instant results – that's the everyday you, always wanting everything at once!

Different people find that they have special aptitudes and their mediumistic power shows itself in different ways; the main types are:

- 'sensitive' mediums
- mediums who 'hear'
- mediums who are spoken through
- mediums who 'see'
- healers
- 'trance' mediums
- physical mediums

'SENSITIVE' MEDIUMS

Sensitive mediums feel the presence of spirits by a kind of vague impression, not related to any particular one of the senses. As with all types of mediumship, the ability can be developed with practice. The sensitive can 'feel' the approach of a spirit, can recognise individual spirits, and can tell if they are good or bad.

MEDIUMS WHO 'HEAR'

The hearing can be of two kinds – either as a voice coming from within the person, or as a voice which appears to be outside, speaking aloud in the 'real' world. Often hearing mediums can hold

conversations with spirits, and other people can join in, using the medium as a kind of telephone.

ϖΕδιυϖS WhO aRΕ SpOKEN thROUGh

This kind of medium often does not hear the voice of the spirit. The spirit uses his or her voice without the medium being conscious of what is being said, which may be quite outside the medium's own knowledge or understanding.

The medium may be perfectly awake while being spoken through, but usually will not remember what has been said.

ϖΕδιυϖS WhO 'SEE'

Some mediums can see spirits, either in a normal waking state or in a trance state. Usually the medium cannot see spirits all the time, but only at special or important times. This is not quite the same as seeing the ghost of a relative, or one trapped in a place which happens to many ordinary people – it is more developed, and seeing mediums can see all kinds of spirits. Sometimes they can describe their appearance in great detail, and can watch crowds of spirits coming and going.

This ability is difficult to develop and should not be forced.

hΕaLΕRS

Not all healers are mediums – many are using subtle energies without the direct help of spirits. Healing mediums call on, and work with, spirits to help cure others. This may be done by touch, or passing the hands over the sick person's aura, or even just by a look. Spiritual surgery, practised in Brazil, (*see* page 64) is a highly advanced practice where the medium is actually able to open up the flesh of a patient with bare hands and conduct an operation

without any normal medical procedures. True spiritual surgeons are very dedicated people who choose their patients carefully and lay down strict purification conditions before they will agree to operate.

'TRANCE' MEDIUMS

Mediums who fall into trances may be in a heightened state, able to use their psychic faculties to answer questions without the aid of spirits, or may simply be reporting what spirits are saying. These conditions often go together in the same person.

PHYSICAL MEDIUMS

Physical mediums are those who produce physical phenomena, such as the movement of objects, causing noises, or producing a fluid called ectoplasm which spirits use to form images of themselves or objects. Ectoplasm is said to be very rare (I have never seen it, and am not convinced it exists), but during the late nineteenth-century fashion for spiritualism there was a great interest in it. Poltergeists (*see* page 13) may work through an unconscious medium to produce physical effects, such as breaking household items.

USES OF MEDIUMSHIP

Here are some common ways in which mediumship is applied:

- bereavement therapy
- messages and information
- obtaining things and events
- prediction
- personal development

They are all useful in their way, but, like anything else, they can become damaging if one becomes too reliant upon them. Let's look at these applications in more detail.

Bereavement therapy

The typical medium that you would find in a Western country during the last hundred years or so is primarily concerned with passing messages from dead souls to their living relatives. During times of trouble, such as during and after the two world wars, many ordinary people, distraught at the senseless loss of their loved ones, turned to mediums for help. I think that mediums can genuinely help people during bereavement, but they must be careful not to encourage dependency.

When you lose someone who is dear to you, you need time to mourn. Mourning involves reflection both on the person who has died, and on what the loss means for your own life. When mourning, we realise all kinds of things about ourselves of which we have hitherto been unaware, and it can be a very distressing, unhappy time. Many people who go to mediums have never really thought deeply about the nature of things; the loss of someone who is close to you can shock you into an awareness that we don't, any of us, have any complete answers to the mysteries of life and death. By working with bereaved people, mediums can help them to come to terms with their loss, and to let their loved ones go.

This process can go wrong, however. Someone who is genuinely looking for answers probably doesn't need to visit a medium more than a few times – the rest is up to them. A person who spends years visiting a medium regularly to plague the dead with questions can become too attached to the process, and what should be a helpful, healing therapy can become a neurotic, stagnant avoidance of the awful fact that we do not have, and cannot get, all the answers to the meaning of existence. A responsible medium must learn to recognise when this is happening, and gently encourage such clients to get on with living and growing.

The same principle applies to people practising mediumship on their own account; they must allow natural processes to take their course, and let go of the person whom they have lost.

MESSAGES AND INFORMATION

Many people go to mediums seeking specific information, such as whether a missing person has actually died, or how someone's disease should be treated. Partial or complete answers may be given. Idle questions, of the 'Who's going to win the lottery?' type, should be ignored. It all depends on the spirit in which the question is asked, and the underlying motive. Sometimes people really do need the answer to a banal material question, and your guide may provide it.

The same thing goes for messages from the dead. Occasionally they have their place – and a pure medium will know when that is – but for the most part they aren't really much help. For instance, there are public meetings where the medium calls out a series of messages – 'I have a message from Jill...' 'Yes,' shouts someone excitedly, 'That's my aunt.' 'Jill says do not worry, dear,' says the medium, and then, 'I keep seeing a dog running around, running around all over the place... is there a dog that has recently passed?' 'It must be my Fido,' calls out someone else.

At worst, this type of meeting is completely fake, but more often the medium is sincere. The people who attend are generally looking for reassurance – a kind of weekly dose of messages from Beyond to keep up their morale. The content of the messages is mainly trivial but can be important to the recipients. Much of it is coming from the people in the room – in other words, it is being 'picked up' by the medium from the individuals who are physically present. And those dead who do come are competing with one another to be heard.

Clearly, it is much better for a medium to conduct sessions one on one with a single client. The attention can then be focussed on the person's particular needs.

OBTAINING THINGS AND EVENTS

People often go to mediums and psychics for solutions to material problems. They want to know if their business project is going to be

successful, say, or, worse still, they want the spirits to help them sell thousands of units of some product. People like this are not looking at their own motives carefully.

If you are in business, you may pray for success, but the most important thing will be to do what you do well – in other words, to sell what people want to buy. Business enterprises of the risk-taking kind can be superb for developing intuition and inner knowledge. Many business people have great insight into human beings; such knowledge is developed over years of struggle. Trying to get spirits to do all the work for you is cheating.

My friend Dilys Guildford (*see* pages 75–82) is a practising medium who says that asking for small things can be a way of getting closer contact with your guides. To test if your psyche is starting to open she recommends the 'parking space' exercise outlined below.

PRACTICE

GETTING A PARKING SPACE

The next time you go out in your car, ask your guides to find you a good place to park. Give them fair warning – start asking before you actually set out, and try to open yourself to their guidance. If you are guided to wait for a while in a certain spot, say, or to turn left down a street, follow this impulse.

With practice, Dilys tells me, you can get very reliable results. It is a process of harmonising yourself with the laws of chance, and allowing the guides to gently ease you into the place where you want to be.

PREDICTION

What would you do if your guide said to you, 'This person is going to die violently in a car crash tomorrow?' Would you gently tell the client that it might be a good idea not to go driving for a few days?

Would you pass on the prediction exactly as you heard it? Or would you say nothing?

Predictions are dangerous things; sometimes it is really much better not to know. When I think of periods of suffering in my own life, I realise that it would only have made things worse if I'd known what was going to happen beforehand.

Sometimes we get very strong messages about the future, however. Here's a true story:

I was living in a small flat in London, and my cousin called to say that she would not be coming to visit me that afternoon as arranged. She had changed her plans, and had decided to stay at home for a few more hours before going directly to Heathrow airport to catch a plane for the United States.

In the evening, she called me from the airport, sounding very distraught. She couldn't explain why, but she wanted to come and stay the night with me instead of getting on the plane. An hour or so later, she arrived, in a distracted state, and I cooked dinner; we didn't talk much about why she hadn't caught the plane, because I could see that she wasn't in the mood to discuss it. Time passed, and I switched the TV on to watch the news, just in time to hear that a PanAm jet had exploded over Scotland, en route from London to New York – what was later to become known as the Locherbie bombing. My cousin went into hysterics – it was the same plane that she was supposed to be on!

She told me that at the airport she had had overpowering visions of fire, death and destruction which had caused her to turn back. She didn't know why, she couldn't explain it, but she had just been certain that she shouldn't get on the plane.

My cousin is a university lecturer in philosophy. She is a confirmed atheist, and likes nothing better than to mock the occult, mysticism and the paranormal. One of her favourite remarks about religion is that it promises 'pie in the sky when you die'. When she had calmed down, I gently asked her how she could account for her premonition; she couldn't.

Naturally, we were both relieved and astounded at her lucky escape,

and she was particularly upset about the people who had died. I had the impression that she had somehow partaken of their experience, and had directly perceived their suffering.

Occasionally we talk of what occurred that night. She is a very honest person, and never denies what happened, but is reluctant to speculate about the causes, and I don't press the point.

There are many similar stories of people having overwhelming premonitions of disaster which help them to save their lives. Sometimes the premonitions come in dreams, and sometimes they just burst straight into our everyday consciousness. It is possible to ignore them, but sensitive people, even if they are rational-minded atheists like my cousin, don't make that mistake.

The point I want to make about prediction is that one must be alert but discreet. If I had had the premonition, it wouldn't have been the same – I might have telephoned her and begged her not to take the plane, but would she have listened? It was really much better that she herself got the message 'direct'.

Personal development

For me, this is what mediumship is really all about – to heal ourselves, both physically and spiritually, and to do the same for others; to cultivate our awareness and understanding of the universe; to recognise that as individuals each of us is uniquely important and meaningful yet, paradoxically, that we are just tiny parts of a vast cosmos. If mediumship is a route to spiritual growth, then it is valid; if it becomes just another rigmarole of confusion and involvement in unimportant things, then it is useless.

5 CHANNELLING

When the iron bird flies, and horses go on wheels,
the Tibetan people will be scattered across the earth ....

Medieval Tibetan prophecy

C hannelling is a modern word which simply means being the
medium through which higher entities can transmit teaching
and assistance to incarnate beings. Thus it refers to what used to be
called 'higher' mediumship, as distinct from the 'Uncle Fred says the
money is behind the settee' type of mediumship.

Channelling is in fashion! Go into any esoteric bookshop these days
and you'll find a wall full of books on channelling (perhaps that's
where you found this book). Workshops on how to find your angel
are springing up everywhere, and people who, a few years ago, were
learning, say, shiatsu and rolfing are now eager to become mediums.
There's nothing wrong with healthy curiosity, but like anything that
suddenly comes into fashion, some people get the wrong end of the
stick. Later in this chapter I will discuss some of the ways in which I
think channelling can go wrong, but first let's look at the positive
side of it.

ANGELS AND GUIDES

There are essentially two types of entity contacted by channellers –
we can call them 'guides' and 'angels'. Guides are beings who are
thought of as having had human existences in the past, but have

now evolved to the point where they will no longer reincarnate on earth. Because guides are ex-humans, as it were, they can talk to us in ways we can understand, and are sympathetic to our frailties. Angels, on the other hand, have never been human beings – it is hard for them to communicate with us directly unless we are in a high, or purified, state of mind. Their power is so strong that they can overwhelm us without meaning to.

It is hard to talk about angels because they are so very different from anything we can understand in our normal states of consciousness; the best we can do is to talk about them in traditional terms, as in religious descriptions and paintings of them. Do they have wings? Yes and no – it is normal to perceive them with wings, but they do not need wings to get around! They are beyond our capacity to understand, and it is silly to get obsessed with trying to describe them in three-dimensional terms. What is important to understand is that, apart from the fallen angels, it is impossible for an angel to do anything wrong or bad. Angels are like principles – love, compassion, health, joy, and so on – which just are; they always behave according to their essential natures.

Carl Jung

Carl Jung was a pioneering psychologist who was a colleague of Sigmund Freud. Becoming unhappy with the direction that Freud's work was taking, Jung founded a school of psychology which grew into what is known today as 'Humanist Psychology'. Humanist psychology is a warm-hearted approach to the study of the mind, and takes mystical and spiritual experiences seriously, rather than regarding them as aberrations, as some other psychological schools are prone to do.

Jung himself was very learned, and became deeply interested in the alchemical writings of the middle ages, believing that a powerful spiritual system was to be found there. Throughout his life, Jung had mystical experiences and frequently had contact with disembodied entities. He developed complex theories to explain these occurrences, and it is well worth reading about them (*see* Further Reading).

Here's Jung's description of the first time he had contact with a guide called Philemon, who had, it seemed, been a pagan on earth:

There was a blue sky, like the sea, covered not by clouds but by flat brown clods of earth. It looked as if the clods were breaking apart and the blue water of the sea were becoming visible between them. But the water was the blue sky. Suddenly there appeared from the right a winged being sailing across the sky. I saw that it was an old man with the horns of a bull. He held a bunch of four keys, one of which he clutched as if he were about to open a lock. He had the wings of the kingfisher with its characteristic colours.

Since I did not understand this dream-image, I painted it in order to impress it on my memory. During the days when I was occupied with the painting, I found in my garden, by the lake shore, a dead kingfisher! I was thunderstruck, for kingfishers are quite rare in the vicinity of Zurich and I have never since found a dead one. The body was recently dead – at the most, two or three days – and showed no external injuries.

Philemon and the other figures of my fantasies brought home to me the crucial insight that there are things in the psyche which I do not produce, but which produce themselves and have their own life. Philemon represented a force which was not myself. In my fantasies I held conversations with him, and he said things which I had not consciously thought. For I observed clearly that it was he who spoke, not I. He said I treated thoughts as if I generated them myself, but in his view thoughts were like animals in the forest, or people in a room, or birds in the air, and added, "If you should see people in a room, you would not think you had made those people, or that you were responsible for them." It was he who taught me psychic objectivity, the reality of the psyche. Through him the distinction was clarified between myself and the object of my thought. He confronted me in an objective manner, and I understood that there is something in me which can say things that I do not know and do not intend, things which may even be directed against me.

C G Jung, *Memories, Dreams, Reflections*, Random House 1961

Jung uses the word 'fantasy' to refer to what mediums tend to think of as the channelling state. He doesn't think of fantasy as being idle imaginations with no relevance to the real world – to him, fantasy states are essential to the mental and spiritual health of the human being. I don't think Jung thought of these guides as really having had human incarnations in the past, however.

Contacting guiðes anð angels

To find the way to open yourself up to these beings, you need to realise that they have always been there, and that you are already in contact with them! Think of times when you have been in terrible trouble, or very ill, or in physical danger. Didn't you ever feel the presence of something good that was helping you?

Here's an exercise you can do to help you remember.

Practice

Remembering your guiðes anð angels

Get some coloured pens and paper and sit or lie down in a comfortable position. If you wish, play some gentle music and light some incense. Cast your mind back across the course of your life. Let the memories of important moments in your life come to you, and draw them or write about them. It doesn't have to be neat and tidy – you can doodle and scrawl as much as you like. Don't judge what comes out, just let it keep on coming. Think about times of crisis – how did you get through them? Try to recall exactly what happened, not just what you were thinking and feeling, but all the things that were going on.

After half an hour or so, you can end the session. Keep what you have written and drawn in a safe place, and look back at

46

it from time to time. Over the next few days, you will probably find that you remember other things about these experiences – you can write these down too, if you wish. As you deepen this 'conversation' with your inner self, relevant ideas, dreams and memories will begin to come to you unbidden. Eventually, beings will appear in your mind whom you will recognise, in your heart of hearts, as old friends.

RECOGNISING YOUR PROTECTION

It's tempting fate a bit to discuss one's own experiences in public, but when I look back at my own life I am astonished at the number of times I've been in really dangerous situations without getting hurt. This doesn't make me feel invulnerable – just very relieved!

When I was eight I was travelling on a train with my mother. Suddenly the carriages were all derailed – there was a pandemonium of screaming, mainly from people who weren't hurt. A table fell on the woman opposite me; we stared at each other, both of us aware of what was going on, yet completely calm. A huge cloud of dust was in the air, shaken out of the seats by the shock of the impact. My mother became hysterical, and scrabbled through her bags looking for our passports.

As we clambered out of the carriages into the fresh air, I felt completely calm and relaxed, observing what was going on with a strange, heightened intensity. I was fascinated by the reactions of people – most had lost their self-control completely. I had the overpowering feeling that they were making things much worse, and that it was all completely unnecessary. A few people, though, remained calm, and got on with the job of helping others out of the wreckage and clearing up the mess. I had the feeling that they were the wise ones, doing God's work, as it were.

Later that year we moved to Toronto in Canada, and I had the great good fortune to join a martial arts club led by a very spiritual man.

I'll never forget a little lecture he once gave to us kids:

'We are non-violent people,' he said, 'We find inner calm within ourselves. If we are ever in an accident, we don't start screaming and having hysterics. We look at what is going on, and help other people who are in distress.'

What does all this have to do with guardian angels? Well, I feel as if the angels were there at the rail accident, helping people to do what had to be done. If everyone in the train had been open to them, there would have been much less distress.

At other times, people have pointed guns at me, and I've been in places where bombs have exploded, or there have been riots. I always feel as if there is a strong, pure channel of wisdom that tells me exactly what to do, and I follow it without question. As long as I am open to this channel, I don't really feel scared. Perhaps I'm just a cold fish, but I prefer to think that angels are helping me!

Should channelling be private?

For me, contact with these good beings is a private thing, not to be chattered about. I have a strong aversion to situations where people swap stories about what their guides and angels are saying. Idle talk is like rubbish that clutters up our minds and makes it harder for us to stay in contact. Naturally, there are times when it is appropriate to discuss them, but I think it is a good idea to err on the side of silence. Silence, not talking, is the way to open your spirit and learn from your guides.

Edgar Cayce

Edgar Cayce was an American born in 1877. From childhood he displayed spiritual gifts, and, like many others, it took him many

years before he understood how he should use them. His life's work, when he found it, took the form of thousands of extraordinary 'readings' which he gave to anyone who came to him. Cayce would lie down on a couch and apparently go to sleep. His wife would then ask him questions on behalf of his client, and a stenographer would record Cayce's answers. The records of these readings are still available today (*see* Useful Addresses).

Many of the problems that clients brought to him were medical, and Cayce would give careful instructions on the cause of the disease and how it might be cured. The 'readings' also produced much curious information about the person's spiritual state, and past histories, including what had happened in previous incarnations on earth. During the readings Cayce spoke in a curious, roundabout way, and it takes a while before you can 'tune in' to the meaning of what is being said.

Cayce did not regard himself as a medium, although he said that he did sometimes contact spirits of the dead and other disembodied beings. He said that he obtained the information from the 'Akashic Records', a part of the unseen world where all the information regarding particular individuals is recorded.

Cayce would lie down on his couch and concentrate on the 'third eye', the point above and between the eyebrows. He would then begin to pray. After a few minutes, he would suddenly see a flash of brilliant white or golden light, which he called the 'go signal'. If he did not see the light, he would abandon the reading. After seeing the light, he would move his hands to his solar plexus, and his breathing would slow down. He would then see himself as a tiny dot, outside his physical body, surrounded by darkness and loneliness. A beam of light would appear, and Cayce would follow it, passing through layers of vague, grotesque forms before emerging on the outskirts of a beautiful city. Entering the city, Cayce would come to a 'hall of records', a vast building without ceilings, where an old man, the keeper of the records, would be waiting for him.

The old man would hand him a book from the library which related to the particular individual for whom the reading was being given. Cayce would find the information in the book, while on the earthly

plane his sleeping body would answer the questions put to him by his wife.

Cayce himself would explain that this vision of the hall of records was a symbolic representation of events that the human mind cannot fully comprehend; he understood that another person accessing this information might have a completely different way of 'seeing' it.

The 'Akashic Records' are a place in inner space where one can find traces of all the actions individuals have taken throughout their existences. To access it, you do not have to see exactly what Cayce saw – it might appear to you as words graven on stone, say, or as an endless wall upon which the course of a person's life is depicted, stretching infinitely forwards towards the future in one direction, and back into the past in the other. Good results can be had if you use a 'conductor' to ask you questions and record the answers, although a very skilled person would not need one.

Edgar Cayce was a simple man who believed that it was his life's work to serve others by using his gifts. He did not use them to get rich, or to get power over other people. He is a good example of how mediums should conduct themselves.

WHEN CHANNELLING GOES WRONG

Because I feel that channelling is essentially a private thing, I don't pay too much attention to publicised channelling. I'm particularly uncomfortable with prophecies – not because I don't think that there can't be genuine prophecies, but because I feel that for every genuine prophecy there are a hundred false ones.

LUCIFER AND AHRIMAN

The great psychic Rudolf Steiner described two evil principles

abroad in the world which he called 'Lucifer' and 'Ahriman'. In essence, he thought of the 'Luciferic' energy as being that which encourages us to get above ourselves. Lucifer encourages us to feel powerful and important, and to think we can become superhuman. He is the inspirer of all movements that believe that the force of the individual is all-important. In the twentieth century, the most notable expression of this was Nazism with its ideology of a Master Race.

Ahriman tells us the opposite. 'You are nothing,' he says, 'You are a mere stone, a piece of material which means nothing except in how it fits in with the rest of creation.' In the twentieth century, the most notable Ahrimanic movement was communism, with its belief in the insignificance of the individual, its gross materialism, and its demand that people sacrifice their own desires in favour of the needs of the mass.

There is no doubt in my mind that these energies reflect real forces which are abroad in the world, and are only too delighted to find people to 'channel' them. It is commonplace in esoteric circles to say that Hitler, for example, was a psychic and a medium.

Temptations

The story of Christ's temptation in the wilderness is symbolic of three major ways in which we can 'go wrong' as we progress along the spiritual path. Here I quote from a modern translation of Matthew's Gospel:

> Jesus was now led by the Spirit up into the desert to be tempted by the Devil. When he had abstained from food for forty days and forty nights and so was starving, the Tempter approached him and said: 'If you are the son of God, order these stones to be turned into loaves.' Jesus replied by citing the Scripture: Man shall not live on bread alone, but on every word that issues from the mouth of God.

> Next, the Devil took Jesus with him to the Holy City, where he made him stand on the cornice of the Temple and said: 'If you are

the son of God, throw yourself down; for the Scriptures say "He will put his angels in charge of thee and they shall hold thee up on their hands, lest thou dash thy foot against a stone." Jesus answered, 'The Scriptures also say "Thou shalt not put the Lord thy God to the proof."'

Again, the Devil took him to a very high mountain and showed him all the kingdoms of the world and their glory. 'All this,' he said, 'I will give you if you prostrate yourself and do me homage.' Then Jesus said to him: 'Satan be gone. For the Scriptures say, "Thou shalt do homage to the Lord thy God and serve him only."' Thereupon the Devil let him be, and Angels came and ministered to his wants.

Matthew 4, from *The Four Gospels*
translated by E V Rieu, Penguin, 1952

Whether or not the 'Devil' appeared to Jesus as described, or whether the story is merely symbolic of a psychological struggle within Jesus, is not a question that concerns me. But I would like to offer my own comments on the relevance that the three temptations have for us.

The first temptation refers to the physical. Apart from it being a general injunction against using miraculous powers in a wrong way, I also take it to mean that we shouldn't get too excited about any unusual abilities that may come to us, such as the power to heal others. When a healer starts to get impressive results, it is quite easy for him or her to get overconfident, and to want to misuse this power in all sorts of idle ways. The power to heal does not belong to the healer in any absolute sense; it comes from Spirit.

The second temptation seems to refer to a more subtle feeling. We sometimes feel that we can just 'go with the flow', and all problems will be sorted out; it is easy to start to think that we are so pure and wonderful that nothing bad can happen to us. Yet the universe is bigger than we are; life has a way of smacking us in the face when we least expect it, however evolved and spiritual we may think we are.

The third temptation always seems to come to people who attain spiritual power, and, perhaps, is the most difficult of all to resist. If a

medium is successful, a great number of people may be drawn to him or her, and it may be that the medium is offered great material opportunities. We only have to think of some of the more prominent gurus and cult leaders to see how they are showered with Rolls Royces, money, buildings and, most tempting of all, political power. Taking advantage of what is offered is a way of letting your little ego usurp what belongs to God.

We could think of the Devil in the wilderness as a channelled entity, but Jesus clearly rejected what he was saying. Channelled messages need not necessarily be helpful or good. Some channelled messages are very silly indeed, so we must exercise our powers of discrimination.

hEALING

*And a woman, having an issue of blood twelve years,
which had spent all her living upon physicians, and
could not be healed of any, came behind him, and
touched the border of his garment: and immediately
the issue of her blood stanched.*

*And Jesus said, Who is it that touched me? And when
all denied, Peter said, and they that were with him,
Master, the multitudes press thee and crush thee.*

*But Jesus said, Some one did touch me: for I perceived
that power had gone forth from me.*

*And when the woman saw that she was not hid, she
came trembling, and falling down before him declared
in the presence of all the people for what cause she
touched him, and how she was healed immediately.*

*And he said unto her, Daughter, thy faith hath made
thee whole; go in peace.*

Luke 8: 43–48

The New Testament tells of many instances of Jesus healing the
sick, sometimes, as in the one quoted above, without even
intending to. God's power, we are told, simply poured out of him
and healed people.

Faith healers seek to emulate this. They exist in most cultures, but
the tradition is particularly strong in Christianity because Jesus

instructed the disciples to go out and heal in God's name. The point of this type of healing is that no knowledge or intermediary is necessary – all is required is the faith that God, the Holy Spirit, or whatever you want to call it, will flow through you and heal the other person.

At the other end of the scale are healers who study their art. Like conventional doctors, they learn a massive amount before they begin to practise. Methods such as homoeopathy, shiatsu, and aromatherapy are all like this; they are disciplines which you study.

Spiritual healing is in between. Most spiritual healers do study the physical and psychic bodies, but they also ask for supernatural help, either from their guides and angels, or simply from their inner selves. In this chapter we will look at some of the esoteric systems used by healers.

Do you need a system at all?

If your intuition is very clear, or the power within you is very strong, perhaps you don't need to know anything of these occult systems. Certainly, there are many healers who have helped others all their lives simply by 'going with the flow'. It is up to you to decide what path you want to take.

The chakra system

Esoteric traditions view the entire universe as a sea of vibrating energy. You can think of it as a spectrum of colours, for instance, or as a series of musical octaves. Here we will look at one way of understanding how these energies relate to each other, called the chakra system, which is a very ancient Indian tradition.

Figure 6.1 depicts the seven chakras within the human psychic bodies. Each chakra is associated with particular endocrine glands and nerve plexuses within the physical body. In most people, these

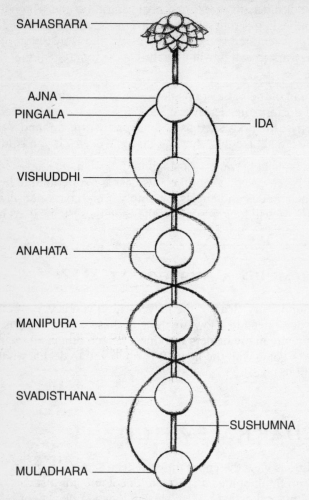

SAHASRARA

AJNA
PINGALA
IDA

VISHUDDHI

ANAHATA

MANIPURA

SVADISTHANA
SUSHUMNA

MULADHARA

Figure 6.1 The chakras, sushumna, ida and pingala

psychic centres are lying dormant and inactive. By undertaking certain spiritual practices, the chakras can be awakened. Spiritual healing can be effected by working on a person's chakras in order to balance and harmonise them.

Let's look at each of the chakras in turn, starting at the bottom and moving up.

Muladhara

This is known as the 'base' or 'root' chakra, and is situated in the region of the perineum, the area between the anus and the genitalia, near the base of the spine. It is associated with the gonads, which in men are the testes and in women the ovaries. Thus, the force of sexual reproduction is linked with the muladhara. Its colour is red, and its psychological force is physical activity. Builders, sportsmen, soldiers and all those who do heavy physical labour are said to have their muladhara 'switched on'.

Svadisthana

This lies a little way up the spine. You can locate it by contemplating the region just above your genitals and below your belly button, and then moving back to the spine. There are other lesser psychic centres nearby with which it is sometimes confused – some martial arts use these other centres for directing force for specific purposes. It is associated with the adrenal glands, which are just above the kidneys. The daily rhythms of energy are associated with this chakra. Its colour is orange, and its psychological force is sensuality and group feeling. People who work in groups, who set great store in domesticity, and who are very sociable are using their svadisthana chakra.

Manipura

This is sometimes said to be in the spine behind the belly button, but I think it is a little higher, behind the solar plexus, which is the point just below the rib cage in the centre of your trunk. The solar plexus is an important nerve centre associated with digestive processes. Manipura also governs the pancreas and gall bladder. Psychologically, manipura governs the intellect, dreaming, and the 'astral body'. Its colour is yellow. People who travel a lot, adore change, and intellectualise are using their manipura chakra. A computer programmer is typically using the manipura.

Anahata

This is in the spine behind the heart. It is the seat of the individuality of a person, or what is sometimes called the soul. Anahata governs the respiratory system and the circulation of the blood. When breathing stops, and the blood stops pumping, death follows quickly. Anahata is associated with the thymus, which is an endocrine organ which helps regulate the immune system, and protects the body from disease. Auto-immune diseases such as AIDS, arthritis and cancer are associated with a malfunction of the thymus. Psychologically, anahata governs the heart forces of love, strength and will. Its colour is green, the colour of life and growth. Business people, leaders, showbusiness stars and all 'big egos' are using the anahata.

Vishuddhi

This is behind the throat, in the spine at the base of the neck. It is associated with the thyroid and parathyroid glands. Too much thyroid hormone makes a person's eyes bulge out, and causes nervousness and irritability; too little causes an enlarged tongue, hoarse voice, puffy eyes and hands and a constant feeling of cold. Vishuddhi governs the long-term memory, knowledge, personal authority and the voice. Its colour is blue. People in positions of authority, such as heads of schools, directors of large organisations, judges, politicians, bishops and doctors are often using their vishuddhi chakra.

Ajna

This is the 'third eye', situated deep within the brain. It is linked with the 'eyebrow centre', a lesser centre located above and between the eyebrows on the forehead. Ajna governs the pituitary gland, a tiny endocrine organ which produces many hormones with multiple effects. An underactive pituitary produces midgets, and an overactive one causes gigantism. Ajna governs the intuition, and deep states of meditation and trance. Its colour is indigo, a very deep, spiritual blue. Poets, designers, some artists, and tender, otherworldly people use this chakra.

Sahasrara

This is said to be the seat of highest consciousness, and is usually depicted as a lotus of a thousand petals on the top of the head. It is associated with the pineal gland, a tiny organ deep within the brain which produces several hormones which are not well understood, including serotonin, which is connected with depression and sleep. Sahasrara's colour is violet. Its psychological force is the creative imagination and the power to change oneself through one's attitudes – myths, magic and archetypes reside here. People who use their sahasrara are relatively rare – they include the great creative artists, visionary leaders and people who change the world.

According to Indian tradition, there are many other psychic centres in and around the body, known as the adharas; the chakras are simply the most important ones.

VARIATIONS

You will find quite a number of variations in ideas about how the chakras work, where they are located, their colours, and so on. I think these variations occur because people differ in the degree to which they have mastered the functions of their own chakras; it can take a whole lifetime, or, perhaps, many lifetimes, to fully awaken and balance all the chakras. Nevertheless, we do not have to be perfect masters in order to work with our chakras – we must just accept that we have imperfect understanding, and continue our training.

The nadis

'Nadi' means a flow, or a current. Traditionally, there are 72,000 nadis in the psychic body of a person. To physical vision, they appear as currents of light around and within the body. Sometimes people call the nadis 'nerves', but they aren't the physical nerves; like the chakras, they exist in the psychic bodies of humans, not the physical. The main nadi is known as the sushumna, which runs up the spinal cord through the chakras.

In the diagram of the chakra centres (Figure 6.1), two secondary nadis are depicted, the ida and pingala. They correspond to the sympathetic and parasympathetic nervous systems in the physical body. To become healthy and balanced, the ida and pingala need to be purified and made harmonious, at which point energy will flow through the sushumna.

Other systems that describe the psychic bodies

Every major spiritual tradition has a system that describes the psychic bodies. The chakra system is a good one because the knowledge has become widely available in the West, and it is not difficult to find people to teach you about it. Other systems include:

- The **Chinese chi system**, used in acupuncture and some martial arts. This depicts a number of meridians around the body which appear to correspond to the nadis in the Indian system. There has been some interesting scientific work on acupuncture; for example, it has been found that an instrument called a 'neuroprobe' which has a sapphire end can be used to identify acupuncture points, and stimulate them. Neuroprobes are used in conventional medicine for physiotherapy on nerve groups.
- The **ancient Egyptian system**, which is only partly known. Referred to in the Egyptian Book of the Dead, it describes a series of spiritual bodies in man which appear to correspond to the chakra system.

It does not matter which system you use, as long as you have access to good teachers – you cannot learn the system's intricacies on your own. One thing that all these systems appear to have in common is the famous esoteric idea, 'As above, so below' – this means that all these systems regard the universe as being a series of patterns within patterns, but having one basic, universal pattern which can be applied to the very smallest things, such as the movements and structure of atoms, right up to the very biggest things, such as galaxies.

The aura

The aura is usually seen as being made up of several 'planes' or 'layers' all of which are interrelated but have specific qualities and

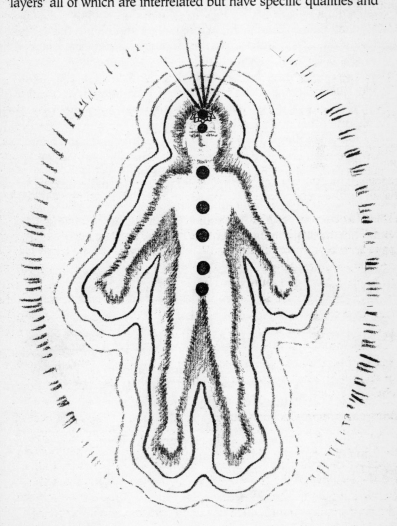

Figure 6.2 The aura

functions. It is easier to see the 'grosser' layers with psychic vision, than the 'higher' layers, and it is the 'grosser' layers which are usually addressed in healing. These correspond to the four lower chakras:

- Muladhara represents the physical body itself.
- Svadisthana represents the 'bioenergy' around the body. This field has many names: prana, chi, ki, orgone, od and bioplasma are just a few of them. The structure of this aura level is identical to the physical body itself – each organ is reproduced in energy form.
- Manipura represents the 'dream body', also known as the 'astral' body. It is sometimes called the mental, or emotional, or astral, but these terms can be confusing because they are sometimes applied to other auric levels. It is that part of the human being that can leave the body in dreams, is very fluid and can change its shape easily. The stories of magicians changing into animals refer to shape changing of this part of the aura. Many disembodied entities have 'dream bodies', as do thought forms and other spiritual flotsam and jetsam.
- The Anahata represents the 'soul body' of the human being. Its harmony or disharmony have direct effects on the 'lower' auric levels.

Note that the chakras are not resident in separate planes, but are present on all levels at the same time.

SENSING The AURA

You don't have to be able to see the aura in order to be a healer – you can sense it in other ways too. It all depends on your own inner path. Many people, however, do find it possible to develop the ability to see auras in great detail.

In the beginning, you will probably see only the lower levels of the aura, and not really be able to distinguish between the different levels. Here are some exercises you can try.

PRACTICE

AURIC ENERGIES WITHIN A GROUP

Make a circle with other people and join hands. Feel the energy from your own aura flowing round the group. Try to feel which direction it is flowing in.

Now, without changing position, get everyone to will the energy flow to stop.

After a while, get everyone to will the energy to start flowing again.

Repeat this procedure a few times, and discuss your experiences; which state feels better, flowing or non-flowing?

PRACTICE

SEEING ENERGY FIELDS

In a darkened room, hold out your hands so the fingers are pointing at one another. Relax, and gaze at the space between them. Do you see anything?

Move your hands closer together. Now move them further apart. What do you see? What do you feel?

Move your attention to the spaces between your fingers. What do you notice?

Move your hands into different positions, around each other, and at different angles to one another. Can you detect any changes?

Most people do find that they begin to see something with a little practice, and almost everyone can feel something. This something is your own energy field – your aura.

The Spirit Surgeons of Brazil

These are the most extraordinary healers working in the world today. With the aid of spiritual guides, these individuals are able to open up people's physical bodies with their bare hands, removing tumors, repairing hernias, and then sealing up the wounds without any of the medical aids you would normally expect. These activities are well documented and have even been successfully filmed. In Brazil, no one is amazed by the spirit surgeons – it is part of everyday life, and people know it works.

Figure 6.3 High-level healing with angelic assistance

A Brazilian friend of mine has been waiting for spiritual surgery for several years. Each time he goes to the healers, they tell him to wait;

it is not the right time. These healers live very dedicated, pure lives, and they often refuse patients. Treatment is given when the healers believe there is a strong likelihood it will succeed.

Heal thyself!

Healers need to be balanced and healthy before they can go out and heal others. Fortunately, there is a wide number of therapies and healing disciplines now available, so you should have little trouble finding workshops and courses where you can learn. You need practical experience – books can help as an introduction, or as a reminder, but you need living, breathing people to teach you properly how it is done.

Disease may originate in the physical body, or in the mind/spirit. Wherever it arises, it will travel to the other part of the person and back again. In spiritual healing we try to treat the whole person, not just the particular symptom that happens to be appearing at the moment.

One mistake that inexperienced healers make is to be overambitious; these energies are real, and healing is not a game. If you try to do too much, it is quite possible that you will 'pick up' the illnesses and imbalances of other people, so do try to be sensible and study under experienced healers.

SELF-DEFENCE

Among other evils which being unarmed brings you, it causes you to be despised.

Machiavelli, *The Prince*

Most of us have a natural 'psychic self-defence system' which we are not really aware of. This helps us to stay out of trouble and keeps us in our everyday states of consciousness. When you start to do any kind of spiritual or psychic work, you start to open yourself up to powerful unseen influences which can be disturbing. Mediums are particularly vulnerable to such disturbances, since they are seeking to make close contact with disembodied entities.

Normally, your best defence against psychic disturbance is to ignore it, by which I mean not giving it more than its due; for most disturbances grow in proportion to the amount of emotional and mental force you are prepared to focus on them. If you do experience psychic disturbance, it is usually your own doing; by careless exploration of the unseen, you can awaken forces which seem to take on a life of their own.

AN ACCIDENTAL INVOCATION

In my late teens I became very keen on psychic experimentation, in company with a girlfriend, Helen, who had been educated at a

Anthroposophical school (a movement founded by Rudolf Steiner, *see* page 50). She was very psychically open, and between us we managed to get into quite a few psychic 'scrapes'. In our eagerness to explore these mysteries, we did not appreciate how unbalanced we were becoming.

There was a little wood near Helen's house, where, it was said, an occult group had invoked demonic entities in the past. One night we thought we would investigate. As we wandered through the wood, we became aware of a non-human presence, powerful and aggressive. It seemed as if it was following us, and we headed for civilisation.

By the time we reached the edge of the wood, Helen was extremely agitated. Suddenly, I saw her spirit begin to rise out of her body – just as it is portrayed in the cinema, it appeared to me that her ghostly form was moving upwards, looking exactly like her physical form, but made of a more tenuous substance. Frightened, I grabbed her, and her 'ghost' shot straight back to her body. Shaken, we hurried home.

For the next few nights, I felt as if something unpleasant was prowling around me. It seemed as if it was trying to 'get into' me, and I started to practise protection exercises, and to pray. At one point, I felt as if I was wrestling with an extremely strong creature which was trying to wrench me away from my body. After a week or so of concentrating on 'normal' everyday activities, the disturbance went away, and has never bothered either of us again.

Was all this just the product of a lively imagination? Maybe, but it seemed very real. What was so shocking was how quickly this entity came when we began to probe, and how long it took to get rid of it.

The star and his demon

A young man I know (I'll call him 'M') has been very successful in showbusiness. A genuinely visionary artist, he divides his time between Los Angeles, London and Sydney, pursuing a glamorous

and lucrative career. He cultivates the persona of magician, and talks openly, and incessantly, of the unseen worlds to everyone he meets.

The executives of the large corporations who employ him are not particularly disturbed by his occult talk, except to wonder occasionally if he is too crazy to be given any responsibility. Their interest is in the commercial exploitation of unusual people, and M, with his dramatic visions of other worlds and talk of entities, gives them what they want. As far as they are concerned, as long as M can produce the artistic results they require, it doesn't matter what he believes.

M says openly that he has a demon guide. When he speaks of it, it sounds so silly that it is easy to think he is putting on an act. In fact, I do not know whether he has actually contacted such an entity, or whether he simply wishes to do so. What is clear, however, is that M is playing a strange and dangerous game with reality. This is his own choice, and not one with which others are entitled to interfere, so long as he doesn't involve other people.

The trouble is that he does involve other people in his fantasies. A circle of unsuccessful actors, writers, film directors and artists has formed around him, hoping, perhaps, that some of his material success will rub off on them. Some of these people are weak and unbalanced, and M is able to exert an unhealthy influence over them. Last year, one of the group lapsed into schizophrenia, and was locked up in a mental institution where he was dosed with a series of damaging medicines with which doctors try to treat the condition. Quite what role M played in his friend's breakdown is not clear, but there is no doubt that M's influence was not having a beneficial effect on him.

M seeks to obtain knowledge of the unseen worlds by taking huge risks. To spend a few hours with him is to be assailed by a whirlwind of crazy mind games – he loves to play with perception, and seeks to create a kind of miasma of confusion around him

through which, he thinks, it is possible to attain higher states of consciousness. One way of describing his activities is to say that he invokes the spirit of chaos.

Crazy Wisdom

In Buddhism, there is a tradition of a spiritual path known as 'Crazy Wisdom', which is suitable for certain unusual people. In Crazy Wisdom, the seekers train themselves to see the universe – in fact, all possible universes – as a game of illusions. On this path, all things are treated as equally illusory, so anything which one normally may think of as bad, horrible or frightening is sought out, the object being to perceive directly that these things are impermanent, to penetrate into their true nature and to lose all fear of them. The stories of Tibetan monks meditating amongst rotting corpses, or visualising themselves being tortured and eaten by demons, relate to this path.

As you might expect, Crazy Wisdom is said to be a dangerous path. What is emphasised is that unless you cultivate compassion and love for all beings, Crazy Wisdom will lead to trouble.

Charles Manson, the notorious leader of the 'Family' which were responsible for the Sharon Tate murders in the late 1960s, seems to have discovered and practised aspects of Crazy Wisdom. Like M, however, he did not cultivate love and compassion. Manson was demonised by the press at the time of the murders, and remains today as the chief bogeyman of the popular imagination in America. He was not present at the Sharon Tate killings, but was judged to have inspired them. What seems to have happened is that he 'created an atmosphere' in which his followers conceived of the idea of the killings themselves. I think we should pity Manson, despite his many crimes; he has spent almost all of his life in the grimmest institutions, and has suffered violent abuse since childhood – enough to make anyone crazy. Send him healing.

The activities of 'witch doctors'

In many societies in Africa, the Caribbean, Latin America and the Far East there are individuals who openly claim to have the power to harm others by magical means. Most of us will not come into contact with them, and if we do, our best course of action is to put a few thousand miles between us and them by going home! Whether or not they have the powers they claim, they certainly have a great capacity for mischief making. Similar individuals are to be found in our society, though they tend to operate a little more discreetly by means of curses, charms, talismans and so on. If you are ever threatened by such a person, don't be frightened – he or she is probably just trying to 'psych you out'. Stand up for yourself, but try to avoid conflict; so long as you are behaving righteously, the individual will suffer far more than you will through his magical activities. On no account be tempted to fight back through occult means – this is merely descending to their level.

Between 1957 and 1971, Haiti was in the hands of a dictator, Papa Doc Duvalier. Papa Doc consciously modelled his oppressive regime on the Nazis, and instituted a secret police force known as the Tonton-macoutes. Voodoo became a state-sanctioned religion, but its dark side was uppermost, and many of the houngans (*see* page 8) were used as agents and informers for the Tonton-macoutes. Ruling by fear, Duvalier used sinister voodoo practices against his people, combining occult practices with very real poisons, such as the 'zombie powder', used to zombify victims, which has been found to contain a powerful nerve agent.

Unconscious attacks

When we live in close proximity to others, we are sometimes subject to unconscious psychological attacks. Let's look at a few common types.

Vampirism

This is a scary name for the everyday phenomenon of people drawing energy from those around them. One often meets them; you can tell what is going on because you always feel so depleted after being with them. Sometimes old people suck energy in this way without meaning to, hence the folk tradition that young people should never sleep in the same bed as their aged relatives. There are times, though, when you might want to give your own energy to someone else in order to help them; this isn't vampirism, since you are giving it freely. The main thing to understand about this type of energy theft is that it works only when both the victim and the victimiser are in very close contact. The solution? Reduce your contact with the person as much as possible, and avoid sharing food, towels, clothes and other intimate domestic objects with them. See 'grounding' on page 78 and the 'protection exercise' on page 18.

Will imposition

Have you ever been the unwilling customer of the 'hard sell'? Aggressive salespeople are sometimes prepared to say and do anything to get you to agree to buy. Sometimes you can actually feel the force of their will bearing down on you. Not only salespeople do this – all sorts of bullies in all walks of life try to impose their wills on others. Don't get agitated or aggressive when this happens – breathe deeply, stay calm, and firmly tell the person you don't want anything to do with it, without leaving any room for argument. Say it with a smile and, if your wits are quick enough, 'label' what they are doing by saying something like, 'I never make purchases when my arm is being twisted', or some similar remark which lets the person know that you are aware of what is going on.

Sly manipulators

These are the sweet talkers who like to appear friendly and helpful,

but who really are not well disposed towards you. They try to create situations where you feel beholden to them, so that they can pretend that any resistance you make later is a betrayal. Just remember that you are always free to make your own choices, and don't be afraid to stand up to emotional blackmail of this kind. They may huff and puff for a while, but in the end they will leave you alone and go looking for a softer target. Check how your own energy feels and stay aware.

General self-defence

It is important to cultivate your intuition, for example by practising the exercise on page 23 regularly. People with bad intentions generally reveal themselves if you are alert; something in their faces, in their speech or in their behaviour will give them away. Recognising that something is wrong is the most important thing – once you have become aware of it, a sensible course of action is usually fairly evident.

Here are some simple 'dos and don'ts' if you encounter people who have bad intentions towards you:

- Don't give strangers or people you feel uncomfortable about any personal articles. In particular, never give them locks of your hair, nail clippings, or personal photographs.
- Don't tell them intimate information about yourself. If you have any private prayers or mantras that you use regularly, don't tell them what they are.
- Don't turn your back on them completely when you are in the same room as they are.
- Do cut yourself off from their influence by folding your arms and crossing your legs when you are talking to them.
- Do wash yourself with cold water after you have left them.

PRACTICE

A PROTECTION RITUAL FOR A ROOM OR A HOUSE

You can use incense and water for complex purification rituals if you are that way inclined, but for those of us who are not, here is an exercise you can do anywhere, any time. The best time for it is just before you go to sleep at night.

Lie down, become conscious of your breathing, and relax.

Visualise the house or room that you are in. Then imagine you are drawing a protective sign in the air that covers one entire side of the building; you can use any symbol you wish, but if you can't think of one, use the pentagram (see diagram).

Figure 7.1 Pentagram

Now visualise the next side of the building and do the same. As you draw the symbol, be aware that this is a powerful protection from outside influences.

Do the same with each remaining side of the building, and then with the roof above you, and the floor beneath you.

Now visualise all the symbols you have drawn. Know that you are safe inside, and that nothing can harm you.

Check for any places that you might not have covered – a window, perhaps, or a part of the building which is on a different level, and imagine yourself drawing the symbol across these too.

If you are still unsure, repeat the process several times. Remind yourself that you are part of the totality of being. You have every right to exist, and your existence is uniquely meaningful and worthwhile. If you believe in God, ask Him to protect you from evil, both that which is within you and that which is outside.

If you wish you can actually perform this exercise physically, standing up and drawing your visualised symbols in the air. If you do this when people may be watching, it can spoil the effect, though, since they may make fun of you. Doing the exercise mentally is just as effective.

8 TRAINING

The heart has its reasons which reason knows nothing of.

Blaise Pascal

Not everyone who reads this book will decide to train to be a full-time medium - it takes aptitude and dedication. While we can all learn to listen to our inner promptings, and to develop a relationship with our guides, it is a big step to start to help strangers with mediumship.

This chapter will advise beginners on how to take steps to deepen their abilities and understanding under the guidance of an experienced teacher. You can't do it all on your own; you need a helping hand from someone who has already learned how to do it. Since we are dealing with matters which are beyond language, there are many things which we can learn only by being shown them – merely reading about them is not enough.

Dilys Guildford is a practising medium who kindly gave up a lot of time to discuss the matters in this book with me. Like all good mediums, she is discreet, and does not like making broad statements which not everyone will understand. While some people come to mediumship with their psychic capacities very open, it takes others years of trying before they develop any kind of sensitivity at all. A good teacher sees the condition that a student is in, and gives appropriate guidance according to his or her needs.

Planchettes and Ouija Boards

Many people have their first contact with spirits by playing these games. There are many variations, but the principle is that a group of people all put their hands on a glass or some other object which moves easily, and then invoke spirits. When the spirits come, the glass moves around a board on which the letters of the alphabet are marked, and spells out the answers to questions.

Dilys says, and I agree with her, that good spirits don't like this game – it is very frustrating for them, since it is a slow process, and they are forced either to answer the questions directly, or to keep silent. These games are also attractive to mischievous entities who have nothing better to do than to play tricks on people's minds.

Psychometry

A better way to start training your sensitivity is to practise psychometry, which means handling an object and opening yourself to any images, smells, sounds or other sensations which come into your mind.

PRACTICE

Simple psychometry

Get a number of objects which you have not handled before, and which belong to someone else. Things which are 'neutral' won't tell you much, so avoid objects which are mass-produced and have never been handled. Suitable things include jewellery which has been worn, ancient artifacts, and personal items which the owner uses frequently.

Put the objects in front of you on a table, and do a basic relaxation procedure to clear your mind. Now pick up one of the objects and attend to what comes into your mind. Don't try to manipulate or interpret what comes – just express it as it first appears. Dilys emphasises that the first answer is the accurate answer – just listen, and be alert.

In the beginning, it is helpful to have someone with you, and to tell them what you experience. If you are alone, you can write down or draw the impressions that you have experienced.

Once you have done this with each of the objects, you can look at the results and try to make sense of them. Often the owner of the object will tell you of some fact which relates to your impression. Keep practising, and it will slowly start to make sense.

Automatic writing

This is a more advanced practice, and not everyone can do it. The idea is that you are allowing yourself to be the vehicle by which a spirit can pass messages to the physical world by means of the written word. For it to work, there are two main conditions:

1 The medium must be psychically 'clear' enough to be able to receive the particular entity.
2 The entity must have something worth saying.

Automatic writing often appears to be nonsense. There are several reasons for this:

● Nonsense writing can be compared with the meaningless chatter you hear on 'talk radio' or from a disc jockey. If the entity is confused and rambling, then the automatic writing will be too.
● Sometimes several entities may be trying to talk at once. You must try to discover why. Often it is because they are competing

to pass messages to various living people who you have been helping.

- An entity may have something important to say, but is encountering barriers in the spiritual realms. It may take many attempts before the message can come through in an intelligible form.

---

practice

Get clean sheets of paper and a variety of pens and crayons. Sit at a tidy table, and perform a protection exercise (*see* pages 18–19). Open yourself. Invite spirits to work through you. Wait until you feel the urge to take up a pen and start to write or draw.

When you are writing, don't be distracted by its content – don't even look at the page. Many mediums find that they write very rapidly, in a sort of frenzy.

When nothing more is coming through, stop, close your eyes and end the session. Wait for a while before examining the pages.

It may take much practice before you are successful at automatic writing, and some people simply find that it is not for them. However, if you are producing material which seems to have some meaning, but you are not sure yet of its significance, keep practising and you may find that over time the meaning becomes clear.

GROUNDING

Dilys emphasises the importance of staying grounded. Once you become sensitive, it is quite easy to start floating about in psychic worlds and become unable to function in every day life. This is an unbalanced state, and can lead to illness. You need to be firmly grounded in this world in order to be in harmony with yourself and the universe.

Figure 8.1 shows a simple exercise to help you stay grounded.

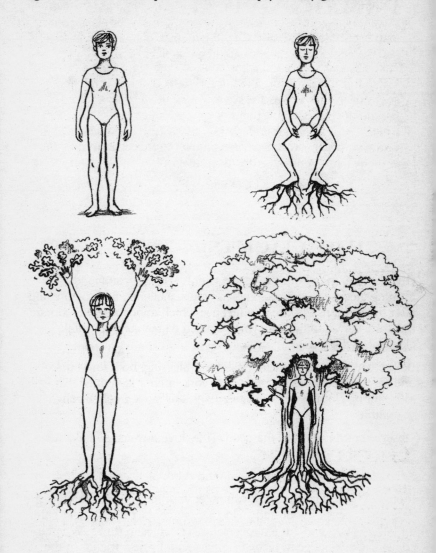

Figure 8.1 Grounding exercise

PRACTICE

GROUNDING YOURSELF

Take off your shoes and stand in your bare feet. Take a glass of water and have a drink. Picture the roots of an oak tree and see your feet becoming the roots. Allow them to sink into the ground and spread out. Bend down and touch your feet, feeling them firmly grounded. As you breathe and stretch upwards, picture your body becoming the trunk, your arms the branches and your fingertips the leaves.

Tune in to your tree, which is you and is safely grounded.

SEEING CLIENTS

One day you may be ready to see clients. Dilys recommends burning incense in the room where you see clients, both before and after the session. Choose any incense which appeals, but if you are not sure, use sandalwood, which is used widely as a spiritual cleanser in the Orient.

Before you begin the session, ask for a blessing, both for yourself and for the person. Dilys prefers to work in bare feet, and wear loose-fitting clothing. This helps energies to move freely through your aura.

Observe courtesies with the dead. They love flowers, so have fresh flowers in the room.

Keep plenty of water in the room, and drink plenty of it.

Prepare yourself so the spirit can meet your mind. Relax, and let go your awareness of your body. Don't try to contact a particular spirit on behalf of your client – allow whatever comes to do so. When it comes, acknowledge it, recognising it mentally as a friend. In the unlikely case that it is clearly not a friend, avoid it, 'using natural feelings', Dilys says.

When the session is over, you need to 'close' it. Although the client has gone, the entities may still be around. If they are very disturbed, if you are a Christian say the Lord's Prayer, or a similar prayer from whatever religion you are closest to.

Ground yourself with the exercise on page 80. Wash the pulse points on your wrists to help bring you back to the everyday world.

Strong, sharp sounds help with closing. Dilys uses Tibetan prayer chimes, which work very well.

Simply chime them together three times and move them around your aura, allowing the tones to continue until they end naturally.

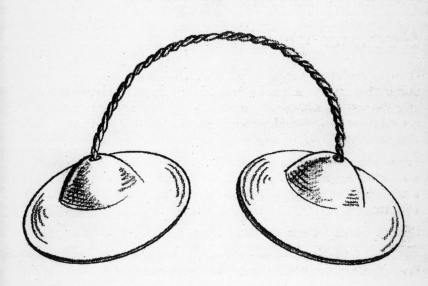

Figure 8.2 Tibetan prayer chimes

finding a teacher

Most of the work you will do when training will be done alone, but it is important to work with others at some stage, to get advice and share your experiences.

It would be useless to recommend any particular organisation or movement. Spirit is a trackless land, and you must rely on your inner guidance to lead you to the right people. The right teacher for one person may not be right for another. In the next chapter we look in some detail at various problems we can experience by following the wrong people – but if you are true to your own heart, they cannot hurt you.

Trust yourself, and the teacher who is right for you will appear.

9 AVOIDING FRAUDS AND SELF-DECEIVERS

You rascals, do you want to live for ever?

Frederick the Great of Prussia, to his troops in battle,
18 June 1757

Although it is 'the most natural thing in the world', mediumship requires the development of subtle and unusual abilities. It is not surprising that some mediums go wrong because of improper motives, such as greed for money and the desire to feel important. Often one comes across mediums with real ability who have somehow become degraded, and 'cheat' in order to maintain their status as mediums.

Anyone can call themselves a medium – you don't have to have any qualifications – and while there are some groups and societies which attempt to set standards, one can have little confidence in these. It is up to you to use your own discrimination and judgement to decide who is sincere and who is not.

While there are undoubtedly out-and-out frauds, most bad mediums do have some ability, which makes it harder to discriminate between them.

Alien abductions and UFOs

Here's the story of something which happened to me not long ago which illustrates the need for caution in these matters.

All around the famous Stonehenge in Wiltshire, England, are a large number of ancient sacred sites, including Silbury Hill, an artificial mound built before 1200 BC. One night I was sitting on top of it, experiencing the extraordinary energies it generates. It is a kind of womb of earth forces, throbbing with enormous power. As I sat there, a strange little man approached me. After a while of exchanging pleasantries, he shyly told me that he was visiting a medium called 'Fat Tracey'.

Fat Tracey had told him that his true love was an alien female, and that if he waited on top of Silbury Hill for long enough, this alien woman would surely come in a spacecraft to take him away from this world to a new life in a far-off galaxy. It was obvious that he was very disturbed by sexual problems, but he was able to laugh at himself, a little.

My heart went out to him; it was clear to me that he had had genuine 'out of time' experiences, but in being convinced that these were alien contacts he had somehow become a victim. He believed that he had somehow failed by not being abducted in a spaceship, and that he couldn't have any girlfriends on earth until 'all this was sorted out'. What was clear was that his interpretation of what was happening was 'disempowering' – it wasn't helping him to take charge of his life, and Fat Tracey was making things worse by telling him to wait for an alien girlfriend.

I have not discussed aliens before now because my opinions on them are likely to upset a lot of New Age people – essentially, I regard the idea that the reports of UFO sightings and alien abductions are of Great Spiritual Significance as mistaken. But before you throw down this book in disgust, give me a chance to explain myself!

First, there is the question of whether it is possible that there are sentient life forms on other planets. The rational speculation in favour of the existence of intelligent aliens goes like this:

- Our sun is an average star – we know that there are many other similar suns in the universe.
- We don't know whether any of these other suns have solar systems because we can't see planets (outside of our own solar system) with telescopes. However, it is not unreasonable to speculate that at least some of these other suns do have solar systems.
- Some of these other solar systems may have planets on which life could have evolved.
- Because of the vast distances in space and the great age of the universe, it is quite unlikely that many evolved life forms would exist at the same time, and that if they did, that they would have enough time to travel far enough across the universe to find other life forms, given that the speed of light is a limiting factor in physical travel.

I accept this argument – in essence, it suggests that while there may be aliens somewhere in the universe at some point in time, it is very unlikely that they could ever make contact with us. But it is not impossible, and if it ever occurs it will be one of the most exciting things that has ever happened.

So much for the speculative argument. Now for the many reports that aliens have already reached the earth in spacecraft, and that they occasionally take people away on them to perform weird experiments. The military, we are told, know about all this and are keeping the information secret:

- It is pretty clear that most of the people making these claims are sincere. They certainly have experienced something very strange – but this doesn't mean that their interpretation of what happened is accurate. It could be that they had inner experiences which they just didn't understand very clearly, as was the case with my friend on Silbury Hill.

- While a fear of the secrecy and malicious intent of the military is quite understandable, it is ridiculous to think that all the armies

of the world have conspired together to keep all this a secret – they just aren't that co-operative with one another. Look at nuclear technology; despite the best efforts of the original nuclear powers, more and more nations have been able develop their own bombs by a combination of spying and original research. A UFO which could travel through space and time would be a valuable prize that every tin-pot dictator would desire – and enemies of the United States would be the first to publicise such a cover-up if they knew of it. By all means distrust the motives of the military, but don't give them too much credit; to me, it is highly unlikely that they could control or suppress an alien invasion of earth, peaceful or not.

There are a number of mediums and New Age teachers who say that these aliens are messengers from angelic beings, that they can be channelled, and that they have important tasks to do with ushering in the New Age on earth. I can find nothing in any of this that rings true – but, as always, check it out for yourself, and draw your own conclusions.

Group pressure

Like bureaucracies, any organised group will tend to want to increase in size and in the demands it makes from its members. Human beings are social animals, and we are naturally inclined to try to fit in with other group members. There's nothing wrong with this in itself, but you should be careful not to give up your own independence entirely.

A couple of famous psychological experiments illustrate how easy it is for things to go wrong. In one test, the subject believes that he or she is an ordinary member of a group; what the person doesn't know is that all the other members have been primed to give a certain answer to a question. The group is shown a card with two shapes on it, and are asked which one is longer; although it is obvious which shape is longer, the primed members all pick the other one – and in the majority of cases, the subject will agree with

them in giving the wrong answer. When the subjects are asked afterwards why they gave the wrong answer, they usually say that although they knew that it was the wrong answer, everyone else was so sure that they felt they had to go along with the majority opinion.

In an American university in the 1960s a group of students was invited to take part in a role-playing game. A wing of a building was reserved for them, and they were divided into two groups, one which was to play the part of prisoners, and the other, prison warders. The intention was to study the group dynamics over an extended period, but after a few days, the experiment started to go badly wrong and had to be closed down – the 'prisoners' were increasingly being subjected to severe punishments, and the warders became more and more authoritarian and aggressive. It was quite a shock to everyone involved to see how these 'normal', educated students could adapt so quickly to their roles. What's the moral of the story? Simply that, given the right circumstances, people can feel justified in doing cruel things in the name of some external authority.

You may well have come across one of the modern cults such as Scientology, the Moonies, the Emin, and the 'Orange People'. They are all unique in various ways, but it is a characteristic of such groups that they feel outside the normal world, and are quite defensive.

Outside their own circles, mediums are not the most popular people. When you become a medium, you take a step outside the norms of modern life, and many people will think you are strange. As an outsider you may experience a good deal of hostility and obstacles – just as anyone else does who is outside the mainstream of their society, whether they are members of a motor cycle gang or a monastery, or the Church of Scientology!

Outsiders often become defensive; if the general public mistrusts or abuses you for your beliefs, it is easy to find yourself thinking that you are better than they are. The first lesson of mediumship is humility – try to remain open and tolerant of others, and avoid feeling superior. If you are a member of a group which starts to encourage you to feel 'special' or 'chosen', look very, very carefully at what is going on.

Even if you are not the member of an organised group, you can still be subject to these pressures. All over the world, New Age conferences and meetings are being held. If you attend them, you'll meet a lot of like-minded people, just as you would if you were a car dealer at an auto convention. Some of these people like to pretend that just because you are interested in spiritual matters, you are an 'old soul', or have 'evolved vibrations'. It is a pleasant feeling to hang around with other people thinking that you are all wonderful, superior beings, but it has nothing to do with true spirituality. Be humble, and think for yourself.

Endorsing other mediums

If you become a practising medium with clients, you are, in a way, setting up in business, and the chances are that you will meet others who are in the same industry. Inevitably, rivalries and competition occurs, and it is easy to start forming alliances and vendettas. Because we New Agers are all supposed to be so enlightened and loving, it can be easy to get into situations where a group of New Age workers pretend to themselves and others that all their work is equally valid and useful. Naturally, if you do know someone who you think can help one of your clients, you should recommend them, but don't simply become a member of a mutual admiration society that unquestioningly endorses each other's work.

The 'end times'

There is nothing like a sense of urgency to keep a group together, and what better way of creating this sense than saying that the world is about to end, or to change dramatically? Cults who await the imminent destruction of the world pop up all the time, and, curiously, if their predictions fail, the group often tends to grow in number. The recent tragic events at Waco, Texas, when so many Branch Davidians under their charismatic leader, David Koresh, lost their lives, is just one example of a phenomenon which has recurred throughout history.

There are many in the New Age movements who, while avoiding cults, live in an excitable state of expectancy of 'end times', or, at least, of imminent catastrophic changes. Such a state of mind seems to me to be worse than the catastrophes themselves. Of course, there are huge changes going on – but when, in truth, have there not been? As one Indian sage likes to say,

'Stop worrying about the atom bomb, and concentrate on exploding the atma bomb.' ('Atma', in Hindu philosophy, means the essential self of a person.)

God-men

Some mystics seek divine knowledge by identifying themselves with God; there is nothing wrong with this if the path is properly understood, but it can lead to delusions of grandeur. There are quite a number of people alive today who claim to be God, and allow their followers to worship them as such.

I refuse to call any man, or woman, God; either we all are parts of God, or none of us is. Look for the truth within yourself – you need no intermediary between your own self and God. Others who tell you to worship them are leading you up the garden path.

Sai Baba is an Indian holy man based in Puttarpathi, a desert village in Andra Pradesh, who claims to be God, and has thousands of devotees, both Western and Indian. He materialises objects from thin air, and there are many reports of him appearing suddenly in other parts of the world, often in several places at the same time. He is a short man with a huge Afro hair-style. I have seen him materialise *vibhuti*, Hindu sacred ash, several times close-up when I visited his ashram in the 1980s and I'm afraid I have come to the conclusion that he is not above using simple stage conjuring tricks. Recently a home video of one of his materialisations has been broadcast which seems to show him palming an object from beneath a tray before producing it as if it had come from thin air.

Figure 9.1 Sai Baba, the God-man of Andra Pradesh

The devotees of Sai Baba with whom I have had contact are a naïve bunch; they seem to think that his materialisations are sufficient evidence of his divinity. Even if it transpires that these 'miracles' are not, or not all, conjuring tricks, all it would show was that he has occult powers, which is not the same thing as being God!

I should say, though, that I had a very pleasant time at Puttarpathi; the food was cheap, the ashram was clean, and I shared a room with two Brahmins from Trinidad who regaled me with hilarious stories of their adventures amongst the holy men of India, as well as teaching me many strange things. So don't take my word for it – go and see Sai Baba for yourself, and make up your own mind.

hidden masters

Since the nineteenth century, a myth has grown up in Western
esoteric circles that there is a group of hidden masters who are
directing the evolution of the world. This idea is due in large part to
the activities of Madame Blavatsky, the unscrupulous nineteenth–
century founder of Theosophy. She describes a Great White
Brotherhood of Masters, beings whose rigorous esoteric training and
absolute purity have given them supernatural powers, and have
made them become immortal. The Masters can materialise in
human form, we are told, or can exist in a more subtle form.
Blavatsky wrote that the head of the brotherhood is the Lord of the
World, who lives in Shamballa in the Gobi Desert. His helpers are
called the Buddha, the Mahachohan, Manu and Maitreya. Manu
has an assistant, Master Morya, who lives on this plane as an
Indian prince in a hidden valley in Tibet. Maitreya has an assistant
called Master Koot Hoomi, with whom Blavatsky claimed to have
many dealings. Other Masters include religious leaders and
philosophers such as Plato, Confucius, Jesus, Francis Bacon, Moses
and so on. The brotherhood works in secret to preserve the destiny
of the cosmos from the evil activities of demonic beings known as
the Lords of the Dark Face.

These ideas have been taken up by many esoteric groups since the
decline of Theosophy, which enjoyed a huge international popularity
in the first half of the twentieth century. They originate in oriental
religious beliefs, but are watered-down, simple-minded,
commercialised, misunderstood versions of them. The hidden
masters myth is a modern construction posing as an ancient belief. If
you want to understand what these stories really signify, you should
look for the answers amongst real Hindu and Buddhist holy men.

Checklist

Overleaf is a list of questions you can ask yourself about any
medium or group you come into contact with. You can ask the same
questions of yourself.

- Are you being flattered?
- Are you being asked for a lot of money?
- Is the medium honest in daily life?
- Is the medium exploiting people with obvious mental illness or personality disorders?
- Is the medium or group trying to control how you live your life?
- Does the medium have a sense of humour?
- Do you like the atmosphere around the person or people?
- In your heart of hearts, do you think the medium is acting selflessly?

Ultimately, it is up to you to trust yourself. Look within yourself for the answers, and don't give up your own inner voice in favour of what others tell you.

USEFUL ADDRESSES

Dilys Guildford

Dilys Guildford, who advised me during the writing of this book, is a practising medium who lives in a wild spot on the coast of Devonshire, England where a village was washed into the sea some 80 years ago. She can be contacted at:

Dilys Guildford
Hallsands Hotel
North Hallsands
Near Kingsbridge
Devon TQ7 2EY
UK
Tel: 01548 511577

White Eagle Lodge

White Eagle Lodge is an international Christian Church founded to give practical expression to the White Eagle teaching:

UK:

White Eagle Lodge
New Lands
Brewells Lane
Liss
Hampshire GU33 7HY
UK
Tel: 01730 893 300

White Eagle Lodge
9 St Mary Abbots Place
Kensington
London
W8 6LS
UK
Tel: 0171 603 7914

USA:
White Eagle Lodge
PO Box 930
Montgomery
Texas 77356
USA

Australia
White Eagle Lodge
Willomee
PO Box 225
Maleny
Queensland 4552
Australia

Spiritualists' National Union (SNU)

The SNU (Hon. President-in-Spirit, Sir Arthur Conan-Doyle) is a registered religious charity with a large number of affiliated Churches in the UK and overseas. Their registered office is:

The Spiritualists' National
   Union
Redwoods
Stansted Hall
Stansted
Essex CM24 8UD
UK
Tel: 01279 816363

Australia
Cronus Centre of Australia
Macgregor Hall
Corner of Childers Street and
   Barry Drive
Canberra City
Australia

Australia

SNU Centre of Western
   Australia
579 Murray Street
Perth 6005
Western Australia

D.M. Jackson
4 Pinetree Gully Road
Burrendah
Perth 6155
Australia

New Zealand

Auckland Spiritual Alliance
120 Carlton Gore Road
PO Box 9477
Newmarket
Auckland 1
New Zealand

Mrs R Wildish
38 Belmont Terrace
Milford 10
Auckland
New Zealand

Mrs B. Hicks
PO Box 366
Paraparaumu
Wellington
New Zealand

Canada

Mrs E. Gerard
Apt 307
1720 Richmond Avenue
Victoria
British Columbia
Canada V8R 4P8

Mrs E.V. Harris
60 Inverlochy Boulevard
Suite 802
Thornhill
Ontario
Canada L3T 4T7

J. Minter
186 Oakmeadow Boulevard
West Hill
Ontario
Canada M1E 4H6

Mrs G.F. Taylor
10 Muirhead Road
704 Willowdale
Ontario
Canada M2J 4P9

Edgar Cayce

Edgar Cayce's psychic readings are preserved and promoted by:

The Association for Research and Enlightenment
PO Box 595
Virginia Beach
VA 23451
USA

Other addresses

Findorn Foundation
Forres
Moray
Near Inverness
Scotland

Barbara Brennan School of Healing
PO Box 2005
East Hampton
NY11937
USA
Tel: (516) 329 0951

FURTHER READING

Alpert, Richard (Baba Ram Dass), *Be Here Now*. Lama Foundation, 1971.

Blackmore, Sue, *Adventures of a Parapsychologist*. Heinemann, 1986.

Blackmore, Sue, *Dying to Live*. Heinemann, 1992.

Blavatsky, H.P., *The Secret Doctrine*. Theosophical Publishing Company, 1888.

Capra, Fritjof, *The Tao of Physics*. Shambhala, 1975.

Cayce, Edgar, T*he Edgar Cayce Series*. Aquarian Press, 1989.

Craze, Richard, *Astral Projection – a beginner's guide*. Hodder and Stoughton, 1996.

Evans-Wentz, W.Y., *The Tibetan Book of the Dead*. Oxford University Press, 1960.

Grof, Stanislav, *Beyond the Brain*. State University of New York, 1985.

Hall, T.H., *The Spiritualists: The Story of Florence Cook and William Crookes*. Helix Press, 1962.

Hoffman, Albert, *LSD: My Problem Child*. Tarcher, 1983.

Huxley, Aldous, *Island*. Perennial Classic, 1972.

James, William, *The Varieties of Religious Experience*. Longman, 1902.

Jung, C.G., *Memories, Dreams, Reflections*. Random House, 1961.

Mowat, Farley, *People of the Deer*. Little, Brown and Company, 1952.

Nyanamoli, Bhikku, *The Life of the Buddha*. Buddhist Publication Society, Kandy 1971.

Shaw, William, *Spying in Guru Land*. Fourth Estate, 1994.

Shure, Edmund, *The Great Initiates*. Rider, 1912.

Steiner, Rudolf, *Rudolf Steiner, An Autobiography*. Anthroposophic Press, 1977.

Von Hoffman, Nicholas, *We Are the People Our Parents Warned Us Against*. Quadrangle, 1968.

Washington, Peter, *Madame Blavatsky's Baboon*. Schocken Books, 1993.

Yates, Frances, *The Rosicrucian Enlightenment*. Arkana, 1986.

Zukav, Gary, *The Dancing Wu Li Masters*. William Morrow and Co., 1979.

GLOSSARY

Akashic Records   a part of 'inner space' where all knowledge of the past is recorded.

astral body   the 'dream body', that part of a person which can travel beyond the body in sleep or trance states.

aura   the non-physical bodies of human beings which are larger than the physical body.

chakra system   a traditional yogic system postulating seven 'psychic centres' within man and, by extension, identifiable in all things at all scales of creation.

chi   Chinese word for unseen energies within human beings.

ectoplasm   physical material produced by mediums which is said to form shapes; may be fraudulent.

Kirlian photography   a process which produces photographs of energy fields surrounding living things.

nadis   in yoga, the 'psychic nerves' in human beings.

ouija board   a parlour game for contacting spirits. Not recommended.

poltergeists   violent energies that occasionally appear around people, particularly adolescents, in a state of great tension.

prana   Sanskrit word for unseen energies within human beings.

psychometry   the art of getting intuitive knowledge by touching objects.

Other titles in this series

Astral Projection 0 340 67418 0   £5.99   Is it possible for the soul to leave the body at will? In this book the traditional techniques used to achieve astral projection are described in a simple, practical way, and Out of the Body and Near Death Experiences are also explored.

Chakras 0 340 62082 X   £5.99   The body's energy centres, the chakras, can act as gateways to healing and increased self-knowledge. This book shows you how to work with chakras in safety and with confidence.

Chinese Horoscopes 0 340 64804 X   £5.99   In the Chinese system of horoscopes, the year of birth is all-important. *Chinese Horoscopes for beginners* tells you how to determine your own Chinese horoscope, what personality traits you are likely to have, and how your fortunes may fluctuate in years to come.

Dowsing 0 340 60882 X   £5.99   People all over the world have used dowsing since the earliest times. This book shows how to start dowsing – what to use, what to dowse, and what to expect when subtle energies are detected.

Dream Interpretation 0 340 60150 7   £5.99   This fascinating introduction to the art and science of dream interpretation explains how to unravel the meaning behind dream images to interpret your own and other people's dreams.

Feng Shui 0 340 62079 X   £5.99   This beginner's guide to the ancient art of luck management will show you how to increase your good fortune and well-being by harmonising your environment with the natural energies of the earth.

Gems and Crystals 0 340 60883 8   £5.99   For centuries gems and crystals have been used as an aid to healing and meditation. This guide tells you all you need to know about choosing, keeping and using stones to increase your personal awareness and improve your well-being.

The Goddess 0 340 68390 2 £5.99   This book traces the development, demise and rebirth of the Goddess, looking at the worship of Her and retelling myths from all over the world.

Graphology 0 340 60625 8 £5.99   Graphology, the science of interpreting handwriting to reveal personality, is now widely accepted and used throughout the world. This introduction will enable you to make a comprehensive analysis of your own and other people's handwriting to reveal the hidden self.

Herbs for Magic and Ritual 0 340 67415 6 £4.99   This book looks at the well-known herbs and the stories attached to them. There is essential information on the use of herbs in essential oils and incense, and on their healing and magical qualities.

I Ching 0 340 62080 3 £5.99   The roots of *I Ching* or the *Book of Changes* lie in the time of the feudal mandarin lords of China, but its traditional wisdom is still relevant today. Using the original poetry in its translated form, this introduction traces its history, survival and modern-day applications.

Interpreting Signs and Symbols 0 340 68827 0 £5.99   The history of signs and symbols is traced in this book from their roots to the modern age. It also examines the way psychiatry uses symbolism, and the significance of doodles.

Love Signs 0 340 64805 8 £5.99   This is a practical introduction to the astrology of romantic relationships. It explains the different roles played by each of the planets, focusing particularly on the position of the Moon at the time of birth.

Meditation 0 340 64835 X £5.99   This beginner's guide gives simple, clear instructions to enable you to start meditating and benefiting from this ancient mental discipline immediately. The text is illustrated throughout by full-colour photographs and line drawings.

Mediumship 0 340 68009 1 £5.99   Whether you want to become a medium yourself, or simply understand what mediumship is about, this book will give you the grounding to undertake a journey of discovery into the spirit realms.

Numerology 0 340 59551 5   £5.99   Despite being scientifically based, numerology requires no great mathematical talents to understand. This introduction gives you all the information you will need to understand the significance of numbers in your everyday life.

Pagan Gods for Today's Man 0 340 691301 1   £5.99 Looking at ancient gods and old stories, this guide explores the social and psychological issues affecting the role of men today. In these pages men of all ages and persuasions can find inspiration.

Paganism 0 340 67013 4   £5.99   Pagans are true Nature worshippers who celebrate the cycles of life. This guide describes pagan festivals and rituals and takes a detailed look at the many forms of paganism practised today.

Palmistry 0 340 59552 3   £5.99   Palmistry is the oldest form of character reading still in use. This illustrated guide shows you exactly what to look for and how to interpret what you find.

Qabalah 0 340 67339 7   £5.99   The Qabalah is an ancient Jewish system of spiritual knowledge centred on the Tree of Life. This guide explains how it can be used in meditation and visualisation, and links it to the chakras, yoga, colour therapy, crystals, Tarot and numerology.

Runes 0 340 62081 1   £5.99   The power of the runes in healing and giving advice about relationships and life in general has been acknowledged since the time of the Vikings. This book shows how runes can be used in our technological age to increase personal awareness and stimulate individual growth.

Shamanism 0 340 68010 5   £5.99   Shamanic technique offers direct contact with Spirit, vivid self-knowledge and true kinship with plants, animals and the planet Earth. This book describes the shamanic way, the wisdom of the Medicine Wheel and power animals.

Spiritual Healing 0 340 67416 4   £5.99   All healing starts with self, and the Universal Power which makes this possible is available to everyone. In this book there are exercises, techniques and guidelines to follow which will enable you to heal yourself and others spiritually.

Star Signs 0 340 59553 1   £5.99   This detailed analysis looks at each of the star signs in turn and reveals how your star sign affects everything about you. This book shows you how to use this knowledge in your relationships and in everyday life.

Tantric Sexuality 0 340 68349 X   £5.99   Tantric Buddhists use sex as a pleasurable path to enlightenment. This guide offers a radically different and exciting new dimension to sex, explaining practical techniques in a clear and simple way.

Tarot 0 340 59550 7   £5.99   Tarot cards have been used for many centuries. This guide gives advice on which sort to buy, where to get them and how to use them. The emphasis is on using the cards positively, as a tool for gaining self-knowledge, while exploring present and future possibilities.

The Moon and You 0 340 64836 8   £5.99   The phase of the Moon when you were born radically affects your personality. This book looks at nine lunar types – how they live, love, work and play, and provides simple tables to find out the phase of your birth.

Visualisation 0 340 65495 3   £5.99   This introduction to visualisation, a form of self-hypnosis widely used by Buddhists, will show you how to practise the basic techniques – to relieve stress, improve your health and increase your sense of personal well-being.

Witchcraft 0 340 67014 2   £5.99   This guide to the ancient religion based on Nature worship answers many of the questions and uncovers the myths and misconceptions surrounding witchcraft. Mystical rituals and magic are explained and there is advice for the beginner on how to celebrate the Sabbats.

Working With Colour 0 340 67011 8   £5.99   Colour is the medicine of the future. This book explores the energy of each colour and its significance, gives advice on how colour can enhance our well-being, and gives ideas on using colour in the home and garden.

Your Psychic Powers 0 340 67417 2   £5.99   Are you psychic? This book will help you find out by encouraging you to look more deeply within yourself. Psychic phenomena such as precognitive dreams, out of body travels and visits from the dead are also discussed in this ideal stepping stone towards a more aware you.

To order this series

All books in this series are available from bookshops or, in case of difficulty, can be ordered direct from the publisher. Prices and availability subject to change without notice. Send your order with your name and address to : Hodder & Stoughton Ltd, Cash Sales Department, Bookpoint, 39 Milton Park, Abingdon, OXON, OX14 4TD, UK. If you have a credit card you may order by telephone – 01235 831700.

Please enclose a cheque or postal order made payable to Bookpoint Ltd, allow the following for postage and packing: UK & BFPO: £1.00 for the first book, 50p for the second book and 30p for each additional book ordered up to a maximum charge of £3.00. OVERSEAS & EIRE: £2.00 for the first book, £1.00 for the second book and 50p for each additional book.

For sales in the following countries please contact:
UNITED STATES: Trafalgar Square (Vermont), Tel: 800 423 4525 (toll-free)
CANADA: General Publishing (Ontario), Tel: 445 3333
AUSTRALIA: Hodder & Stoughton (Sydney), Tel: 02 638 5299

A MEDIUM QUESTIONS
SPIRITUALISM